95

The Ideas That Birthed
the Reformation

Martin Luther

WHITAKER
HOUSE

All Scripture quotations are taken from the King James Version of the Holy Bible.

Publisher's Note: This new edition from Whitaker House has been slightly updated for the modern reader. Some words, expressions, and sentence structure have been revised for clarity and readability.

95:
The Ideas That Birthed the Reformation

ISBN: 978-1-62911-961-8
eBook ISBN: 978-1-62911-962-5
Printed in the United States of America
© 2017 by Whitaker House

Whitaker House
1030 Hunt Valley Circle
New Kensington, PA 15068
www.whitakerhouse.com

Library of Congress Cataloging-in-Publication Data

Names: Luther, Martin, 1483–1546, author. | Luther, Martin, 1483–1546. Disputatio pro declaratione virtutis indulgentiarum. English. | Whitaker House, editor.
Title: 95 : the ideas that birthed the Reformation / by Martin Luther.
Other titles: Ninety-five : the ideas that birthed the Reformation
Description: New Kensington, PA : Whitaker House, 2017. | Includes bibliographical references.
Identifiers: LCCN 2017031112 (print) | LCCN 2017030707 (ebook) | ISBN 9781629119618 (trade pbk. alk. paper) | ISBN 9781629119625 (E-book) | ISBN 9781629119618 (paperback)
Subjects: LCSH: Theology—Early works to 1800. | BISAC: RELIGION / Christian
Church / History. | RELIGION / Christianity / Lutheran. | RELIGION / Christian Theology / History.
Classification: LCC BR331 .E5 2017b (ebook) | LCC BR331 (print) | DDC 261.2—dc23
LC record available at https://lccn.loc.gov/2017031112

2 3 4 5 6 7 8 9 10 11 12 **Ⱳ** 24 23 22 21 20 19 18 17

CONTENTS

A WORD FROM THE EDITOR

In 1517, a thriving new industry was sweeping northern Germany. Begun a few centuries earlier, its reappearance in the sixteenth century was perhaps the cleverest abuse of church power to date. Church officials strapped for cash but being pressured by Pope Leo X to contribute to the restoration of buildings in the Vatican, primarily St. Peter's Basilica, decided to offer remission from the punishment for sins, or "indulgence," to German believers in return for a commensurate amount of money. The sale of indulgences grew until it was widely preached that, with enough money, you could buy yourself out of Purgatory itself, or at least out of inconvenient required religious observances such as Lenten fasts.

This slick church salesmanship of indulgences incensed one young priest, who believed that faithful Christians were being manipulated and the Word of God misinterpreted. A faithful student, he wrote a pamphlet comprised of ninety-five claims that he hoped would inspire scholarly debate on the subject. That pamphlet was titled *Disputation of Dr. Martin Luther Concerning Penitence and Indulgences*, but it went down in history simply as "The 95 Theses."

Most historians believe that Martin Luther never intended for this argument to go public. It was written in Latin, the language of scholars, and it was pinned to the door of the Wittenberg Castle Church. In that day, the church door served as a "bulletin board" of sorts, and posting to it was a common method for inviting other scholars to engage in theological debate. Luther's pamphlet, however, would not be just another piece of paper flapping in the wind. Someone copied it down, had it translated into common German, and then distributed it among the general public with the help of a recent local invention—the printing press. Although Luther tried to retrieve his work, the damage was done. As an important agricultural trading hub, whatever happened in Wittenberg was soon spread far and wide. Within weeks, the theses had spread throughout Germany, and within months, all of Europe.

Many identified with Luther's sense of outrage at the corruption and deceit practiced by the church. Once a respected academic like Luther dared to question a practice of the Roman Catholic Church, it was much easier for less-educated Germans to join in the criticism. Luther's writings eventually made their way to the pope, who responded by attacking Luther and eventually excommunicating him from the Catholic Church. Luther's one pamphlet lit the spark that led to the Protestant Reformation. His influence on the church almost cannot be overestimated.

Five hundred years later, Whitaker House presents each of Luther's 95 Theses paired with an excerpt from his many writings. Not every excerpt was directly written in defense of the accompanying thesis, but we have endeavored to select passages in which Luther was expounding on the same subject. Where further explanation was thought necessary to contextualize his words, a footnote was included. Small substitutions have been made to aid in continuity, style, and readability, but for the most part, what you will find on these pages is the original text from the indicated translations.

We hope you will find *95: The Ideas That Birthed the Reformation* to be an accessible and fascinating look into the ideas and expressions of this groundbreaking priest who stood up for the truth of God's Word and the grace of the gospel—and made history.

—Whitaker House

SOURCE MATERIAL

EXCERPTS TAKEN FROM THE FOLLOWING WORKS BY MARTIN LUTHER:

Martin Luther, *First Principles of the Reformation or the Ninety-Five Theses and the Three Primary Works of Dr. Martin Luther* (London: John Murray, 1883).

This work includes:

Disputation of Dr. Martin Luther Concerning Penitence and Indulgences, translated from Latin by Rev. R. S. Grignon.

"To the Christian Nobility of the German Nation Respecting the Reformation of the Christian Estate," translated from German by C. A. Buchheim, Ph. D.

"Concerning Christian Liberty," translated from Latin by Rev. R. S. Grignon.

"On the Babylonish Captivity of the Church," translated from Latin by Rev. R. S. Grignon.

Martin Luther, *The Sermons of Martin Luther*, Vol. 1–VII, translated by John Nicholas Lenker, originally published in 1909 in English by The Luther Press, Minneapolis, MN.

This work includes the following sermons:

"The Parable of the Sower"

"Christ Our Great High Priest"

"Christ's Holy Sufferings"

"The Twofold Use of the Law & Gospel"

"Enemies of the Cross of Christ"

"Of the Office of Preaching"

Martin Luther, *A Commentary on St. Paul's Epistle to the Galatians*, new abridged translation by Theodore Graebner, DD (Grand Rapids, MI: Zondervan, 1939).

Martin Luther, *Luther's Commentary on the First Twenty-Two Psalms*, translated by Dr. Henry Cole, (Sunbury, PA: Lutherans in All Lands Co., 1903).

Martin Luther, *Luther's Works, Vol. 32: Career of the Reformer II* (Minneapolis: Fortress Press, 1958).

Martin Luther, *Table Talk*, translated by Williams Hazlitt, Esq. (Philadelphia: The Lutheran Publication Society, 1848).

INTRODUCTORY LETTER

To the most Reverend Father in Christ and most illustrious Lord, Albert, Archbishop and Primate of the Churches of Magdeburg and Mentz, Marquis of Brandenburg, etc., his lord and pastor in Christ, most gracious and worthy of all fear and reverence—Jesus.

The grace of God be with you, and whatsoever it is and can do.

Spare me, most reverend Father in Christ, most illustrious Prince, if I, the very dregs of humanity, have dared to think of addressing a letter to the eminence of your sublimity. The Lord Jesus is my witness that, in the consciousness of my own pettiness and baseness, I have long put off the doing of that which I have now hardened my forehead to perform, moved thereto most especially by the sense of that faithful duty that I feel I owe to your most reverend Fatherhood in Christ. May your Highness then, in the meanwhile, deign to cast your eyes on one grain of dust, and, in your pontifical clemency, to understand my prayer.

Papal indulgences are being carried about, under your most distinguished authority, for the building of St. Peter's. In respect of these I do not so much accuse the extravagant sayings of the preachers, which I have not heard, but I grieve at the very false ideas that the people conceive from them, and that are spread abroad in common talk on every side—namely, that unhappy souls believe that, if they buy letters of indulgences, they are assured of their salvation; also, that, as soon as they have thrown their contribution into the chest, souls forthwith fly out of purgatory; and furthermore, that so great is the grace thus conferred, that there is no sin so great—even, as they say, if, by an impossibility, any one had violated the Mother of God—but that it may be pardoned; and again, that by these indulgences a man is freed from all punishment and guilt.

O gracious God! It is thus that the souls committed to your care, most excellent Father, are being taught unto their death, and a most severe account, which you will have to render for all of them, is growing and increasing. Hence, I have not been able to keep silent any longer on this subject, for by no function of a bishop's office can a man become sure of salvation, since he does not even become sure through the grace of God infused into him, but the apostle bids us to be ever working out our salvation in fear and trembling. (See Philippians 2:12.) Even the righteous man—says Peter—shall scarcely be saved. (See 1 Peter 4:18.) In fine, so narrow is the way that leads to life, that the Lord, speaking by the prophets Amos and Zachariah, calls those who are to be saved brands snatched from the burning, and our Lord everywhere declares the difficulty of salvation.

Why then, by these false stories and promises of pardon, do the preachers of them make the people to feel secure and without fear? Since indulgences confer absolutely no good on souls as regards salvation or holiness, but only take away the outward penalty that was wont of old to be canonically imposed.

Finally, works of piety and charity are infinitely better than indulgences, and yet they do not preach these with such display or so much zeal; nay, they keep silence about them for the sake of preaching pardons. And yet it is the first and sole duty of all bishops that the people should learn the gospel and Christian charity: for Christ nowhere commands that indulgences should be preached. What a dreadful thing it is then, what peril to a bishop, if, while the gospel is passed over in silence, he permits nothing but the noisy outcry of indulgences to be spread among his people, and bestows more care on these than on the gospel! Will not Christ say to them: "Straining at a gnat, and swallowing a camel"? (See Matthew 23:24.)

Beside all this, most reverend Father in the Lord, in that instruction to the commissaries that has been put forth under the name of your most reverend Fatherhood, it is stated—doubtless without the knowledge and consent of your most reverend Fatherhood—that one of the principal graces conveyed by indulgences is that inestimable gift of God, by which man is reconciled to God, and all the pains of purgatory are done away with; and further, that contrition is not necessary for those who thus redeem souls or buy confessional licenses.

But what can I do, excellent Primate and most illustrious Prince, save to entreat your reverend Fatherhood, through the Lord Jesus Christ, to deign to turn on us the eye of fatherly care, and to suppress that advertisement altogether and impose on the preachers of pardons another form of preaching, lest perchance someone should at length arise who will put forth writings in confutation of them and of their advertisements, to the deepest reproach of your most illustrious Highness. It is intensely abhorrent to me that this should be done, and yet I fear that it will happen, unless the evil be speedily remedied.

This faithful discharge of my humble duty I entreat that your most illustrious Grace will deign to receive in a princely and bishop-like spirit—that is, with all clemency—even as I offer it with a most faithful heart, and one most devoted to your most reverend Fatherhood, since I too am part of your flock. May the Lord Jesus keep your most reverend Fatherhood for ever and ever. Amen.

From Wittenberg, on the eve of All Saints, in the year 1517.

If it so please your most reverend Fatherhood, you may look at these Disputations, that you may perceive how dubious a matter is that opinion about indulgences, which they disseminate as if it were most certain.

To your most reverend Fatherhood,
Martin Luther

THE 95 THESES
OR
DISPUTATION OF DR. MARTIN LUTHER
CONCERNING PENITENCE AND INDULGENCES

In the desire and with the purpose of elucidating the truth, a disputation will be held on the underwritten propositions at Wittenberg, under the presidency of the Reverend Father Martin Luther, Monk of the Order of St. Augustine, Master of Arts and of Sacred Theology, and ordinary Reader of the same in that place. He therefore asks those who cannot be present and discuss the subject with us orally, to do so by letter in their absence. In the name of our Lord Jesus Christ. Amen.

OUR LORD AND MASTER JESUS CHRIST IN SAYING: "*REPENT YOU*," ETC., INTENDED THAT THE WHOLE LIFE OF BELIEVERS SHOULD BE PENITENCE.

This perverted notion about works is invincible when sincere faith is wanting. For those sanctified doers of works cannot but hold it, till faith, which destroys it, comes and reigns in the heart. Nature cannot expel it by her own power; nay, cannot even see it for what it is, but considers it as a most holy will. And when custom steps in besides, and strengthens this depravity of nature, as has happened by means of impious teachers, then the evil is incurable, and leads astray multitudes to irreparable ruin. Therefore, though it is good to preach and write about penitence, confession, and satisfaction, yet if we stop there and do not go on to teach faith, such teaching is without doubt deceitful and devilish. For Christ, speaking by His servant John, not only said: "*Repent you;*" but added: "*for the kingdom of heaven is at hand*" (Matthew 3:2).

For not one Word of God only, but both, should be preached; new and old things should be brought out of the treasury, as well the voice of the law, as the word of grace. The voice of the law should be brought forward, that men may be terrified and brought to a knowledge of their sins, and thence be converted to penitence and to a better manner of life. But we must not stop here; that would be to wound only and not to bind up, to strike and not to heal, to kill and not to make alive, to bring down to hell and not to bring back, to humble and not to exalt. Therefore the word of grace, and of the promised remission of sin, must also be preached, in order to teach and set up faith; since, without that word, contrition, penitence, and all other duties, are performed and taught in vain.

There still remain, it is true, preachers of repentance and grace, but they do not explain the law and the promises of God to such an end, and in such a spirit, that men may learn whence repentance and grace are to come. For repentance comes from the law of God, but faith or grace from the promises of God, as it is said: *"Faith comes by hearing, and hearing by the word of God"* (Romans 10:17). Whence it comes, that a man, when humbled and brought to the knowledge of himself by the threats and terrors of the law, is consoled and raised up by faith in the divine promise. Thus, *"weeping may endure for a night, but joy comes in the morning"* (Psalm 30:5). Thus much we say concerning works in general, and also concerning those which the Christian practices with regard to his own body.

From "Concerning Christian Liberty."

THIS WORD CANNOT BE UNDERSTOOD OF SACRAMENTAL PEN-
ANCE, THAT IS, OF THE CONFESSION AND SATISFACTION WHICH
ARE PERFORMED UNDER THE MINISTRY OF PRIESTS.

I shall speak of the sacrament of penance. By the tracts and disputations that I have published on this subject I have given offense to very many, and have amply expressed my own opinions. I must now briefly repeat these statements in order to unveil the tyranny that attacks us on this point as unsparingly as in the sacrament of the bread. In these two sacraments, gain and lucre find a place, and therefore the avarice of the shepherds has raged to an incredible extent against the sheep of Christ; while even baptism, as we have seen in speaking of vows, has been sadly obscured among adults, that the purposes of avarice might be served.

The first and capital evil connected with this sacrament is, that they have totally done away with the sacrament of penance itself, leaving not even a vestige of it. Whereas this, like the other two sacraments, consist of the word of the divine promise on one side and of our faith on the other, they have overthrown both of these. They have adapted to the purposes of their own tyranny Christ's Word of promise, when He says: *"Whatsoever you shall bind on earth shall be bound in heaven"* (Matthew 16:19); and *"Whatsoever you shall bind on earth shall be bound in heaven: and whatsoever you shall loose on earth shall be loosed in heaven*" (Matthew 18:18); and again: "*Whosoever sins you remit, they are remitted to them; and whosoever sins you retain, they are retained*" (John 20:23). These words are meant to call forth the faith of penitents, that they may seek and obtain remission of their sins. But these men, in all their books, writings, and discourses, have not made it their object to explain to Christians the promise conveyed in these words, and to show them what they ought to believe, and how much consolation they might have, but to establish in the utmost length, breadth and depth their own powerful and violent tyranny.

At last some have even begun to give orders to the angels in heaven, and to boast with an incredible frenzy of impiety that they have received the right to rule in heaven and on earth, and have the power of binding even in heaven. Thus, they say not a word about the saving faith of the people, but talk largely of the tyrannical power of the pontiffs; whereas Christ's words do not deal at all with power, but entirely with faith.

From "On the Babylonish Captivity of the Church."

IT DOES NOT, HOWEVER, REFER SOLELY TO INWARD PENITENCE; NAY SUCH INWARD PENITENCE IS NAUGHT, UNLESS IT OUTWARDLY PRODUCES VARIOUS MORTIFICATIONS OF THE FLESH.

Let us examine the subject on a deeper and less simple principle. Man is composed of a twofold nature, a spiritual and a bodily. As regards the spiritual nature, which they name the soul, he is called the spiritual, inward, new man; as regards the bodily nature, which they name the flesh, he is called the fleshly, outward, old man. The apostle speaks of this: *"Though our outward man perish, yet the inward man is renewed day by day"* (2 Corinthians 4:16). The result of this diversity is that in the Scriptures, opposing statements are made concerning the same man; the fact being that in the same man these two men are opposed to one another; the flesh lusting against the spirit, and the spirit against the flesh. (See Galatians 5:17.)

We first approach the subject of the inward man that we may see by what means a man becomes justified, free, and a true Christian; that is, a spiritual, new, and inward man. It is certain that absolutely none among outward things, under whatever name they may be reckoned, has any weight in producing a state of justification and Christian liberty, nor, on the other hand, an unjustified state and one of slavery. This can be shown by an easy course of argument.

What can it profit the soul that the body should be in good condition, free and full of life; that it should eat, drink, and act according to its pleasure; when even the most impious slaves of every kind of vice are prosperous in these matters? Again, what harm can ill-health, bondage, hunger, thirst, or any other outward evil do to the soul, when even the most pious of men, and the freest in the purity of their conscience, are harassed by these things? Neither of these states of things has to do with the liberty or the slavery of the soul.

And so it will profit nothing that the body should be adorned with sacred vestments, or dwell in holy places, or be occupied in sacred offices, or pray, fast, and abstain from certain meats, or do whatever works can be done through the body and in the body. Something widely different will be necessary for the justification and liberty of the soul, since the things I have spoken of can be done by any impious person, and only hypocrites are produced by devotion to these things. On the other hand, it will not at all injure the soul that the body should be clothed in profane raiment, should dwell in profane places, should eat and drink in the ordinary fashion, should not pray aloud, and should leave undone all the things abovementioned, which may be done by hypocrites.

And, to cast everything aside, even speculations, meditations, and whatever things can be performed by the exertions of the soul itself, are of no profit. One thing, and one alone, is necessary for life, justification, and Christian liberty; and that is the most holy Word of God, the gospel of Christ, as He says: *"I am the resurrection, and the life: he that believes in Me, though he were dead, yet shall he live"* (John 11:25); and also *"If the Son therefore shall make you free, you shall be free indeed"* (John 8:36); and *"Man shall not live by bread alone, but by every word that proceeds out of the mouth of God"* (Matthew 4:4).

From "Concerning Christian Liberty."

THE PENALTY THUS CONTINUES AS LONG AS THE HATRED
OF SELF—THAT IS, TRUE INWARD PENITENCE—CONTINUES;
NAMELY, TILL OUR ENTRANCE INTO THE KINGDOM OF HEAVEN.

If we were pure from all sin and were inflamed with perfect love, both for God and for our neighbor, then we should indeed be righteous and holy through love, and God could require no more of us. This is not done in this present life but is deferred until the life to come. We do here receive the gift and firstfruits of the Spirit, so that we begin to love (see Romans 8:23), though very slightly. But if we loved God truly and perfectly, as the law of God requires (see Deuteronomy 6:5; Matthew 22:37), then we would be as contented with poverty as with wealth, with pain as with pleasure, and with death as with life. Anyone who could love God truly and perfectly would not last long in this life but would be swallowed up by this love.

But at this time, human history is so corrupt and drowned in sin that it cannot have any right sense or thought of God. It does not love God but hates Him with a deadly hatred. Therefore, as John says, it is "not that we loved God, but that he loved us and sent his Son as an atoning sacrifice for our sins." (See 1 John 4:10.) And as Paul said earlier, Christ "*loved me, and gave Himself for me*"

(Galatians 2:20; see also 4:4–5). Being redeemed and justified by the Son, we begin to love. As Paul says in Romans 8:3–4: *"What the law could not do, in that it was weak through the flesh, God sending His own Son in the likeness of sinful flesh, and for sin, condemned sin in the flesh. That the righteousness of the law might be fulfilled in us"*— that is, that they might begin to be fulfilled.

Thus, in verse 13, when Paul says, *"For if you live after the flesh, you shall die: but if you through the Spirit do mortify the deeds of the body, you shall live we are to live by the Spirit,"* he is showing how he wants us to understand the words serve one another in love. He had not forgotten the doctrine of justification, for when he tells them to live by the Spirit, he is plainly denying that works justify us. He is saying, in effect, "When I speak about fulfilling the law, I do not mean that you are justified by the law. I mean that there are two opposing captains in you—the Spirit and the sinful nature. God has stirred up a battle in your bodies. I require of you nothing but to follow the Spirit as your captain and guide, and so also so resist the sinful nature, for that is all you are able to do. Obey the Spirit, and fight against the sinful nature. Therefore, when I teach you to observe the law and exhort you to love one another, you are not to think that I am taking back what I have said about the doctrine of faith and now attribute justification to the law or to love. What I mean is that you should live by the Spirit and not fulfill the desires of the sinful nature."

The desires of the sinful nature are not yet dead in us but spring up again and again and fight against the Spirit. No believers are so good that their sinful nature will not bite and devour, or at least omit some of what love commands. Even at the first attack they cannot deny themselves but get angry with their neighbor, desiring to be revenged; they hate their neighbor as an enemy, or at least do not love him as much as they should and as this commandment requires. This happens even to believers.

From *A Commentary on St. Paul's Epistle to the Galatians.*

5

THE POPE HAS NEITHER THE WILL NOR THE POWER TO REMIT ANY PENALTIES, EXCEPT THOSE THAT HE HAS IMPOSED BY HIS OWN AUTHORITY, OR BY THAT OF THE CANONS.

I say then, neither pope, nor bishop, nor any man whatever has the right of making one syllable binding on a Christian man, unless it is done with his own consent. Whatever is done otherwise is done in a spirit of tyranny; and thus the prayers, fastings, almsgiving, and whatever else the pope ordains and requires in the whole body of his decrees, which are as many as they are iniquitous, he has absolutely no right to require and ordain; and he sins against the liberty of the church as often as he attempts anything of the kind. Hence it has come to pass that while the churchmen of the present day are strenuous defenders of church liberty, that is, of wood, stone, fields, and money (for in this day things ecclesiastical are synonymous with things spiritual), they yet, by their false teaching, not only bring into bondage the true liberty of the church, but utterly destroy it; yea, more than the Turk himself could; contrary to the mind of the apostle, who says, *"Be not ye the servants of men"* (1 Corinthians 7:23). We are indeed made servants of men when we are subjected to their tyrannical ordinances and laws.

This wicked and flagitious tyranny is aided by the disciples of the pope, who distort and pervert to this end the saying of Christ: *"He that heareth you heareth me"* (Luke 10:16). They swell out these words into a support for their own traditions; whereas this saying was addressed by Christ to the apostles when they were going forth to preach the gospel, and therefore ought to be understood as referring to the gospel alone. These men, however, leave the gospel out of sight, and make this saying fit in with their own inventions. Christ says: *"My sheep hear my voice"* (John 10:27) and *"they know not the voice of strangers"* (John 10:5). For this cause the gospel was bequeathed to us, that the pontiffs might utter the voice of Christ; but they utter their own voice, and are determined to be heard.

The apostle also says of himself that he was not sent to baptize, but to preach the gospel; and thus no man is bound to receive the traditions of the pontiff, or to listen to him, except when he teaches the gospel and Christ; and he himself ought to teach nothing but the freest faith. Since, however, Christ says: *"He that heareth you heareth me,"* why does not the pope also hear others? Christ did not say to Peter alone: "he who hears thee." Lastly, where there is true faith there must also, of necessity, be the word of faith. Why then does not the unbelieving pope listen to his believing servant who has the word of faith? Blindness, blindness reigns among the pontiffs.

From "On the Babylonian Captivity of the Church."

THE POPE HAS NO POWER TO REMIT ANY GUILT, EXCEPT BY DECLARING AND WARRANTING IT TO HAVE BEEN REMITTED BY GOD; OR AT MOST BY REMITTING CASES RESERVED FOR HIMSELF; IN WHICH CASES, IF HIS POWER WERE DESPISED, GUILT WOULD CERTAINLY REMAIN.

But you will ask, "What is this word, and by what means is it to be used, since there are so many words of God?" I answer, the apostle Paul (see Romans 1) explains what it is, namely, the gospel of God, concerning His Son, incarnate, suffering, risen, and glorified through the Spirit, the Sanctifier. To preach Christ is to feed the soul, to justify it, to set it free, and to save it, if it believes the preaching. For faith alone, and the efficacious use of the Word of God, bring salvation. *"If thou shalt confess with thy mouth the Lord Jesus, and shalt believe in thine heart that God hath raised him from the dead, thou shalt be saved"* (Romans 10:9). And again, *"Christ is the end of the law for righteousness to every one that believeth"* (verse 4); and, *"The just shall live by faith"* (Romans 1:17). For the Word of God cannot be received and honored by any works, but by faith alone. Hence it is clear that, as the soul needs the Word alone for life and justification, so it is justified by faith alone and not by any works. For if it could be justified by any other means, it would have no need of the Word, nor consequently of faith.

But this faith cannot consist at all with works; that is, if you imagine that you can be justified by those works, whatever they are, along with it. For this would be to halt between two opinions, to worship Baal, and to kiss the hand to him, which is a very great iniquity, as Job says. Therefore, when you begin to believe, you learn at the same time that all that is in you is utterly guilty, sinful, and damnable; according to that saying: *"All have sinned, and come short of the glory of God"* (Romans 3:23). And also: *"There is none righteous, no, not one: there is none that understandeth, there is none that seeketh after God. They are all gone out of the way, they are together become unprofitable; there is none that doeth good, no, not one"* (Romans 3:10–12). When you have learned this, you will know that Christ is necessary for you, since He has suffered and risen again for you, that, believing on Him, you might by this faith become another man, all your sins being remitted, and you being justified by the merits of another, namely, of Christ alone.

From "Concerning Christian Liberty."

God never remits any man's guilt, without at the same time subjecting him, humbled in all things, to the authority of his representative the priest.

Contrition, though it has been completely exposed to wicked and pestilent doctrines, has yet given less occasion to tyranny and the love of gain. But confession and satisfaction have been turned into the most noted workshops for lucre and ambition. To speak first of confession. There is no doubt that confession of sins is necessary, and is commanded by God. *"And were baptized of* [John] *in Jordan, confessing their sins"* (Matthew 3:6). *"If we confess our sins, he is faithful and just to forgive us our sins…. If we say that we have not sinned, we make him a liar, and his word is not in us"* (1 John 1:9–10). If the saints must not deny their sin, how much more ought those who are guilty of great or public offenses to confess them. But the most effective proof of the institution of confession is given when Christ tells us that an offending brother must be told of his fault, brought before the church, accused, and finally, if he neglect to hear the church, excommunicated. He "hears" when he yields to reproof, and acknowledges and confesses his sin.

The secret confession, however, which is now practiced, though it cannot be proved from Scripture, is, in my opinion, highly satisfactory, and useful or even necessary. I could not wish it not to exist; nay, I rejoice that it does exist in the church of Christ, for it is the one great remedy for afflicted consciences. When, after laying open our conscience to a brother, and unveiling all the evil that lay hidden there, we receive from the mouth of that brother the word of consolation sent forth from God; receiving which by faith we find peace in a sense of the mercy of God, who speaks to us through our brother. What I protest against is the conversion of this institution of confession into a means of tyranny and extortion by the bishops. They reserve certain cases to themselves as secret, and then order them to be revealed to confessors named by themselves, and thus vex the consciences of men; filling the office of bishop, but utterly neglecting the real duties of a bishop, which are to preach the gospel and to minister to the poor. Nay, these impious tyrants principally reserve to themselves the cases that are of less consequence, while they leave the greater ones everywhere to the common herd of priests—cases such as the ridiculous inventions of the bull "*In Coena Domini.*" That their wicked perverseness may be yet more manifest, they do not reserve those things that are offenses against the worship of God, against faith, and against the chief commandments, but even approve and teach them; such as those journeyings hither and thither on pilgrimage, the perverted worship of saints, the lying legends of saints, the confidence in and practice of works and ceremonies; by all which things the faith of God is extinguished and idolatry is nourished, as it is at this day. The pontiffs we have nowadays are such as those whom Jeroboam established at Dan and Beersheba as ministers of the golden calves—men who are ignorant of the law of God, of faith, and of all that concerns the feeding of the sheep of Christ, and who only thrust their own inventions upon the people by terror and power.

From "On the Babylonish Captivity of the Church."

THE PENITENTIAL CANONS ARE IMPOSED ONLY ON THE LIVING, AND NO BURDEN OUGHT TO BE IMPOSED ON THE DYING, ACCORDING TO THEM.

It has been of advantage, however, that this unction[1] has been made extreme, for, thanks to this, it has been of all sacraments the least harassed and enslaved by tyranny and thirst for gain; and this one mercy has been left to the dying, that they are free to be anointed, even if they have not confessed or communicated. Whereas if it had continued to be of daily employment, especially if it had also healed the sick, even if it had not taken away sins, of how many worlds would not the pontiffs by this time have been masters—they who, on the strength of the one sacrament of penance, and by the power of the keys, and through the sacrament of orders, have become such mighty emperors and princes? But now it is a fortunate thing that, as they despise the prayer of faith, so they heal no sick, and, out of an old rite, have formed for themselves a new sacrament.

Let it suffice to have said thus much concerning these four sacraments. I know how much it will displease those who think that we are to enquire about the number and use of the sacraments,

---

1. Sacrament of anointing the sick.

not from the holy Scriptures, but from the See of Rome—as if the See of Rome had given us those sacraments, and had not rather received them from the schools of the universities, to which, without controversy, it owes all that it has. The tyranny of the popes would never have stood so high if it had not received so much help from the universities; for among all the principal Sees, there is scarcely any other that has had so few learned bishops. It is by force, fraud, and superstition alone that it has prevailed over the rest; and those who occupied that see a thousand years ago are so widely diverse from those who have grown into power in the interim, that we are compelled to say that either the one or the other were not pontiffs of Rome.

There are besides some other things, which it may seem that we might reckon among sacraments—all those things, namely, to which a divine promise has been made, such as prayer, the Word, the cross. For Christ has promised in many places to hear those that pray; especially in the eleventh chapter of the Gospel of St. Luke, where He invites us to prayer by many parables. Of the Word He says: *"Blessed are they that hear the word of God, and keep it"* (Luke 11:28). And who can reckon how often He promises succor and glory to those who are in tribulation, suffering, and humiliation? Nay, who can count up all the promises of God? For it is the whole object of all Scripture to lead us to faith; on the one side urging us with commandments and threatenings, on the other side inviting us by promises and consolations. Indeed all Scripture consists of either commandments or promises. Its commandments humble the proud by their requirements; its promises lift up the humble by their remissions of sin.

From "On the Babylonish Captivity of the Church."

9

Hence the Holy Spirit acting in the pope does well for us, in that, in his decrees, he always makes exception of the article of death and of necessity.

One should also abolish certain punishments inflicted by the canon law, especially the interdict[2], which is doubtless the invention of the evil one. Is it not the mark of the devil to wish to better one sin by more and worse sins? It is surely a greater sin to silence God's word and service, than if we were to kill twenty popes at once, not to speak of a single priest or of keeping back the goods of the church. This is one of those gentle virtues that are learned in the spiritual law; for the canon or spiritual law is so called because it comes from a spirit—not however from the Holy Spirit, but from the evil spirit.

Excommunication should not be used except where the Scriptures command it: that is, against those that have not the right faith, or that live in open sin, and not in matters of temporal goods. But now the case has been inverted; each man believes and lives as he pleases, especially those that plunder and disgrace others with excommunications; and all excommunications are

---

2. A censure, or prohibition, excluding the faithful from participation in certain holy things

now only in matters of worldly goods. For which we have no one to thank but the holy canonical injustice.

The other punishments and penalties—suspension, irregularity, aggravation, re-aggravation, deposition, thundering, lightning, cursing, damning and what not—all these should be buried ten fathoms deep in the earth, that their very name and memory may no longer live upon earth. The evil spirit, who was let loose by the spiritual law, has brought all this terrible plague and misery into the heavenly kingdom of the holy church, and has thereby brought about nothing but the harm and destruction of souls, that we may well apply to it the words of Christ: *"But woe unto you, scribes and Pharisees, hypocrites! for you shut up the kingdom of heaven against men: for ye neither go in yourselves, neither suffer ye them that are entering to go in"* (Matthew 23:13).

From "To the Christian Nobility of the German Nation Respecting the Reformation of the Christian Faith."

10

THOSE PRIESTS ACT WRONGLY AND UNLEARNEDLY, WHO, IN THE CASE OF THE DYING, RESERVE THE CANONICAL PENANCES FOR PURGATORY.

It has seemed best, however, to consider as sacraments, properly so called, those promises which have signs annexed to them. The rest, as they are not attached to signs, are simple promises. It follows that, if we speak with perfect accuracy, there are only two sacraments in the church of God, Baptism and the Bread; since it is in these alone that we see both a sign divinely instituted and a promise of remission of sins. The sacrament of penance, which I have reckoned along with these two, is without any visible and divinely appointed sign; and is nothing else, as I have said, than a way and means of return to baptism. Not even the schoolmen can say that penitence agrees with their definition; since they themselves ascribe to every sacrament a visible sign, which enables the senses to apprehend the form of that effect which the sacrament works invisibly. Now penitence or absolution has no such sign; and therefore they will be compelled by their own definition either to say that penitence is not one of the sacraments, and thus to diminish their number, or else to bring forward another definition of a sacrament.

From "On the Babylonish Captivity of the Church."

THOSE TARES ABOUT CHANGING OF THE CANONICAL PENALTY
INTO THE PENALTY OF PURGATORY SEEM SURELY TO HAVE BEEN
SOWN WHILE THE BISHOPS WERE ASLEEP.

The forgiveness of guilt, the heavenly indulgence, is granted to no one on account of the worthiness of their contrition over their sins, nor on account of any works of satisfaction, but only on account of faith in the promise of God: *"Whatsoever thou shalt loose...shall be loosed"* (Matthew 16:19). Although contrition and good works are not to be neglected, one is nevertheless not to build upon them, but only upon the sure words of Christ, who pledges to you that when the priest frees you, you shall be free. Your contrition and works may deceive you, and the devil will quickly annihilate them in death and assaults, but Christ your God will not lie to you, nor will he waver; neither will the devil turn Christ's word aginst him. And if you build upon them with a firm faith, you will be standing on the rock against which the gates and all the powers of hell cannot prevail.

It follows further that the forgiveness of guilt is not within the province of any human office or authority, be it pope, bishop, priest, or any other. Rather, it depends exclusively upon the Word of Christ and your own faith. For Christ did not intend to base our comfort, our salvation, our confidence on human words or deeds but only upon Himself, upon His words and deeds. Priests, bishops, and popes are only servants who hold before you the Word of Christ, upon which you should rely and sit upon with a firm faith as upon a solid rock. Then the Word will keep you, and your sins will have to be forgiven. Therefore, the Word is not honored because of the priests, bishops, or pope; but priests, bishops, and pope are to be honored because of the Word, as those who bring to you the word and message of your God that you are freed from sins.

From "On the Babylonish Captivity of the Church."

12

FORMERLY THE CANONICAL PENALTIES WERE IMPOSED NOT AFTER, BUT BEFORE ABSOLUTION, AS TESTS OF TRUE CONTRITION.

In the Old Covenant, the priest with his sacrifices and sprinklings of blood effected merely as it were an external absolution, or pardon, corresponding to the childhood stage of the people. The recipient was permitted to move publicly among the people; he was externally holy and as one restored from excommunication. He who failed to obtain absolution from the priest was unholy, being denied membership in the congregation and enjoyment of its privileges; in all respects he was separated like those in the ban today.

But such absolution rendered no one inwardly holy and just before God. Something beyond that was necessary to secure true forgiveness. It was the same principle that governs church discipline today. He who has received no more than the remission, or absolution, of the ecclesiastical judge will surely remain forever out of heaven. On the other hand, he who is in the ban of the church is hell-bound only when the sentence is confirmed at a higher tribunal. I can make no better comparison than to say that it was the same in the old Jewish priesthood as now in the papal priesthood, which, with its loosing and binding, can prohibit or permit only external communion among Christians. It is true, God required such measures in the time of the Jewish dispensation that He might restrain by fear; just as now He sanctions church discipline when rightly employed, in order to punish and restrain the evil-doer, though it has no power in itself to raise people to holiness or to push them into wickedness.

But with the priesthood of Christ is true spiritual remission, sanctification, and absolution. These avail before God—God grant that it be true of us—whether we be outwardly excommunicated, or holy, or not. Christ's blood has obtained for us pardon forever acceptable with God. God will forgive our sins for the sake of that blood so long as its power shall last and its intercession for grace in our behalf, which is forever. Therefore, we are forever holy and blessed before God. This is the substance of the text.

From "Christ Our Great High Priest."

13

THE DYING PAY ALL PENALTIES BY DEATH, AND ARE ALREADY
DEAD TO THE CANON LAWS, AND ARE BY RIGHT RELIEVED
FROM THEM.

> *And when he putteth forth his own sheep, he goeth before
> them, and the sheep follow him: for they know his voice. And
> a stranger will they not follow, but will flee from him: for they
> know not the voice of strangers.* (John 10:4–5)

In this text there are two thoughts worthy of note: the liberty
of faith, and the power to judge. You know that our soul-murder-
ers have proposed to us that what the councils and the learned
doctors decide and decree, that we should accept, and not judge for
ourselves whether it is right or not. They have become so certain
of the infallibility of the councils and doctors that they have now
established the edict, publicly seen, that if we do not accept what
they say, we are put under the ban.

Remember well that the sheep have to pass judgment upon
that which is placed before them. They should say: We have Christ

as our Lord and prefer His Word to the words of any man, or to those of the angels of darkness. We want to examine and judge for ourselves whether the pope, the bishops, and their followers do right or not. For Christ says here that the sheep judge and know which is the right voice and which is not. Now let them come along. Have they decreed anything? We will examine whether it is right, and according to our own judgment interpret that which is a private affair for each individual Christian, knowing that the authority to do this is not human, but divine. Even the real sheep flee from a stranger and hold to the voice of their shepherd.

Now the papists object to judgment being passed upon any of their works; for this reason they have intruded and taken from us the sword that we might use for such a purpose. Also, they dictate that we must accept, without any right of judgment, whatever they propose. And it has almost come to such a pass that whenever the pope breathes they make an article of faith out of it, and they have proclaimed that the authorities have the right to pass such laws for their subjects as they desire, independent of the judgment of the latter. These conditions mean ruin to the Christians, so much so that a hundred thousand swords should be desired for one pope. This they know very well, and they cling hard to their laws. If they would permit unbiased judgment, their laws would be set aside and they would have to preach the pure Word; but such a course would reduce the size of their stomachs and the number of their horses.

Therefore, be ye aroused by this passage of Scripture to hew to pieces and thrust through everything that is not in harmony with the gospel, for it belongs to the sheep to judge, and not to the preachers. You have the authority and power to judge everything that is preached; that and nothing less. If we have not this power, then Christ vainly said to us in Matthew 7:15: *"Beware of false prophets, which come to you in sheep's clothing, but inwardly they are ravening wolves."* We could not beware if we had not the power to judge, but were obliged to accept everything they said and preached.

From "On the Office of Preaching."

14

Cast your sins from yourself upon Christ, believe with a festive spirit that your sins are His wounds and sufferings, that He carries them and makes satisfaction for them, as Isaiah 53:6 says: *"the Lord hath laid on him the iniquity of us all,"* and St. Peter in his first Epistle 2:24: *"Who his own self bare our sins in his own body on the tree"* of the cross; and St. Paul in 2 Corinthians 5:21: *"[God] hath made him to be sin for us, who knew no sin; that we might be made the righteousness of God in him."* Upon these and like passages you must rely with all your weight, and so much the more the harder your conscience martyrs you. For if you do not take this course, but miss the opportunity of stilling your heart, then you will never secure peace, and must yet finally despair in doubt. For if we deal with our sins in our conscience and let them continue within us and be cherished in our hearts, they become much too strong for us to manage and they will live forever. But when we see that they are laid on Christ and He has triumphed over them by His resurrection and we fearlessly believe it, then they are dead and have become as nothing. For upon Christ they cannot rest, there they are swallowed up by His resurrection, and you see now no wound, no pain, in Him, that is, no sign of sin. Thus St. Paul speaks in Romans 4:25, that He was delivered up for our trespasses and was raised for our justification; that is, in His sufferings He made known our sins and also crucified them; but by His resurrection He makes us righteous and free from all sin, even if we believe the same differently.

From "Christ's Holy Sufferings."

15

THIS FEAR AND HORROR IS SUFFICIENT BY ITSELF, TO SAY NOTHING OF OTHER THINGS, TO CONSTITUTE THE PAINS OF PURGATORY, SINCE IT IS VERY NEAR TO THE HORROR OF DESPAIR.

When man, conscious of his failure to keep God's command, is constantly urged by the Law to make payment of his debt, and is confronted with nothing but the terrible wrath of God and eternal condemnation, he cannot but sink into despair over his sins. Such is the inevitable consequence where the Law alone is taught with a view to attaining heaven thereby. The vanity of such trust in works is illustrated in the case of the noted hermit mentioned in *Vitae Patrum* (Lives of the Fathers). For over seventy years this hermit had led a life of utmost austerity, and had many followers. When the hour of death came he began to tremble, and for three days was in a state of agony. His disciples came to comfort him, exhorting him to die in peace since he had led so holy a life. But he replied: "Alas, I truly have all my life served Christ and lived austerely; but God's judgment greatly differs from that of men."

Note, this worthy man, despite the holiness of his life, has no acquaintance with any article but that of the divine judgment according to the Law. He knows not the comfort of Christ's gospel.

After a long life spent in the attempt to keep God's commandments and secure salvation, the Law now slays him through his
own works. He is compelled to exclaim: "Alas, who knows how
God will look upon my efforts? Who may stand before him?" That
means, to forfeit heaven through the verdict of his own conscience.
The work he has wrought and his holiness of life avail nothing.
They merely push him deeper into death, since he is without the
solace of the gospel, while others, such as the thief on the cross
and the publican, grasp the comfort of the gospel, the forgiveness
of sins in Christ. Thus sin is conquered; they escape the sentence
of the Law, and pass through death into life eternal.

From "The Twofold Use of the Law & Gospel."

16

Hell, purgatory, and heaven appear to differ as despair, almost despair, and peace of mind differ.

> *Return, O Lord, deliver my soul: oh save me for thy mercies' sake.* (Psalm 6:4)

The psalmist beautifully shows the power of hope while he sets nothing before his eyes but the mercy of God: saying, *"for thy mercies' sake."* As if he had said, not for my merits, for I have none; as is sufficiently manifest from this my terror at Your anger, from my perturbation of heart, and from the vexation of my bones and of my soul: therefore, save me for Your mercy's sake: that the glory and praise of Your mercy may be exalted in my salvation unto all eternity. For though I be unworthy of being delivered and saved, yet You are worthy of being praised, glorified, and loved, to all eternity: and yet, You cannot be praised, nor can Your mercy be glorified, unless there be some whom You shall save from death and deliver from hell.

And here at one blow, and in one moment perishes all the prating of those who talk about meriting grace by works of congruity, and gaining heaven by works of condignity; and who, by an incredible madness, prepare to meet the intolerable judgement of God, by the works of their own righteousness. And therefore David, at the end of this psalm, attacks such with a fiery zeal of spirit, inveighing against them in words addressed especially to them; saying, *"Depart from me, all ye workers of iniquity"* (verse 8). So that this truth stands firm and certain—*"oh save me for thy mercies' sake"*: for my iniquity is found to be unto death and hell, my righteousness is all vanished, my strength has failed, and my merit has come to naught. Blessed man that I shall be, if I be but allowed to breathe unto, and rest in, thy mercy!

Here therefore, we are taught, that as we ought not to presume at all concerning ourselves, so, we ought not by any means to despair of the mercy of God; but ought, however unworthy we may be, to call upon that mercy to save us from the power of death and hell. For what sins or what evils can there be so great, that they should lead thee to despair, when you heart from this Scripture, that no one ought to be led to despair when under the feelings of death and hell, where there must of necessity be the greatest of all sins and evils?

From *A Commentary on the First Twenty-Two Psalms.*

17

WITH SOULS IN PURGATORY IT SEEMS THAT IT MUST NEEDS BE
THAT, AS HORROR DIMINISHES, SO CHARITY INCREASES.

Now if you are not able to believe,…then you should pray
to God for faith. For this is a matter in the hands of God that
is entirely free, and is also bestowed alike at times knowingly, at
times secretly, as was just said on the subject of suffering.

But now bestir yourself to the end: first, not to behold Christ's
sufferings any longer; for they have already done their work and
terrified you; but press through all difficulties and behold His
friendly heart, how full of love it is toward you, which love constrained Him to bear the heavy load of your conscience and your
sin. Thus will your heart be loving and sweet toward Him, and
the assurance of your faith be strengthened. Then ascend higher
through the heart of Christ to the heart of God, and see that Christ
would not have been able to love you if God had not willed it in
eternal love, to which Christ is obedient in His love toward you;
there you will find the divine, good father heart, and, as Christ
says, be thus drawn to the Father through Christ. Then will you
understand the saying of Christ in John 3:16: *"God so loved the
world, that he gave his only begotten Son,"* etc. That means to know
God aright, if we apprehend Him not by His power and wisdom,

which terrify us, but by His goodness and love; there our faith and confidence can then stand unmovable and man is truly thus born anew in God.

From "Christ's Holy Sufferings."

18

Think of the honor and the glory Christ's righteousness brings even to our bodies! How can this poor, sinful, miserable, filthy, polluted body become like unto that of the Son of God, the Lord of Glory? What are you—your powers and abilities, or those of all men, to effect this glorious thing? But Paul says human righteousness, merit, glory, and power have nothing to do with it. They are mere filth and pollution, and condemned as well. Another force intervenes, the power of Christ the Lord, who is able to bring all things into subjection to Himself. Now, if He has power to subject all things unto Himself at will, He is also able to glorify the pollution and filth of this wretched body, even when it has become worms and dust. In His hands it is as clay in the hands of the potter, and from the polluted lump of clay He can make a vessel that shall be a beautiful, new, pure, glorious body, surpassing the sun in its brilliance and beauty.

Through baptism Christ has taken us into His hands, actually that He may exchange our sinful, condemned, perishable, physical lives for the new, imperishable righteousness and life He prepares for body and soul. Such is the power and the agency exalting us to marvelous glory—something no earthly righteousness of the Law could accomplish. The righteousness of the Law leaves our bodies to shame and destruction; it reaches not beyond physical existence. But the righteousness of Christ inspires with power, making evident that we worship not the body but the true and living God, who does not leave us to shame and destruction, but delivers from sin, death, and condemnation, and exalts this perishable body to eternal honor and glory.

From "Enemies of the Cross of Christ."

19

Nor does this appear to be proved, that they are sure and confident of their own blessedness, at least all of them, though we may be very sure of it.

Who also hath made us able ministers of the new testament; not of the letter, but of the spirit: for the letter killeth, but the spirit giveth life. (2 Corinthians 3:6)

This passage relative to spirit and letter has in the past been wholly strange language to us. Indeed, to such extent has man's nonsensical interpretation perverted and weakened it that I, though a learned doctor of the holy Scriptures, failed to understand it altogether, and I could find no one to teach me. And to this day it is unintelligible to all popedom. In fact, even the old teachers—Origen, Jerome, and others—have not caught Paul's thought. And no wonder, truly! For it is essentially a doctrine far beyond the power of man's intelligence to comprehend. When human reason meddles with it, it becomes perplexed. The doctrine is wholly unintelligible to it, for human thought goes no farther than the Law and the Ten Commandments. Laying hold upon these it confines itself to them. It does not attempt to do more, being governed by the principle that unto Him who fulfils the demands of the Law, or commandments, God is gracious. Reason knows nothing about the wretchedness of depraved nature. It does not recognize the fact that no man is able to keep God's commandments; that all are under sin and condemnation; and that the only way whereby help could be received was for God to give His Son for the world, ordaining another ministration, one through which grace and reconciliation might be proclaimed to us. Now, he who does not understand the sublime subject of which Paul speaks cannot but miss the true meaning of his words. How much more did we invite this fate when we threw the Scriptures and Saint Paul's epistles under the bench, and, like swine in husks, wallowed in man's nonsense! Therefore, we must submit to correction and learn to understand the apostle's utterance aright.

From "The Twofold Use of the Law & Gospel."

20

THEREFORE THE POPE, WHEN HE SPEAKS OF THE PLENARY
REMISSION OF ALL PENALTIES, DOES NOT MEAN SIMPLY OF ALL,
BUT ONLY OF THOSE IMPOSED BY HIMSELF.

I must not forget the poor convents. The evil spirit, who has troubled all estates of life by human laws, and made them unendurable, has taken possession of some abbots, abbesses, and prelates, and led them so to rule their brothers and sisters, that they do but go soon to hell, and live a wretched life even upon earth, as is the case with all the devil's martyrs. For they have reserved in confession all, or at least some, deadly sins, which are secret, and from these no brother may on pain of excommunication and on his obedience absolve another. Now we do not always find angels everywhere, but men of flesh and blood, who would rather incur all excommunication and menace than confess their secret sins to a prelate or the confessor appointed for them; consequently they receive the sacrament with these sins on their conscience, by which they become irregular and suffer much misery. Oh blind shepherds! Oh foolish prelates! Oh ravenous wolves! Now I say that in cases where a sin is public and notorious, it is only right that the Prelate alone should punish it, and such sins and no others he may reserve and except for himself; over private sins he has no authority, even though they may be the worst that can be committed or imagined. And if the prelate excepts these, he becomes a tyrant and interferes with God's judgment.

Accordingly I advise these children, brothers and sisters: if your superiors will not allow you to confess your secret sins to whomsoever you will, then take them yourself, and confess them to your brother or sister, to whomsoever you will; be absolved and comforted, and then go or do what your wish or duty commands; only believe firmly that you have been absolved, and nothing more is necessary. And let not their threats of excommunication, or irregularity, or what not, trouble or disturb you; these only apply to public or notorious sins, if they are not confessed: you are not touched by them. How canst thou take upon thyself, thou blind prelate, to restrain private sins by thy threats? Give up what thou canst not keep publicly; let God's judgment and mercy also have its place with thy inferiors. He has not given them into thy hands so completely as to have let them go out of His own; nay, thou hast received the smaller portion. Consider thy statutes as nothing more than thy statutes, and do not make them equal to God's judgment in heaven.

From "To the Christian Nobility of the German Nation Respecting the Reformation of the Christian Estate."

21

THUS THOSE PREACHERS OF INDULGENCES ARE IN ERROR
WHO SAY THAT, BY THE INDULGENCES OF THE POPE, A MAN IS
LOOSED AND SAVED FROM ALL PUNISHMENT.

Until the present we have been in the Passion week and have celebrated Good Friday in the right way: now we come to Easter and Christ's resurrection. When man perceives his sins in this light and is completely terror-stricken in his conscience, he must be on his guard that his sins do not thus remain in his conscience, and nothing but pure doubt certainly come out of it; but just as the sins flowed out of Christ and we became conscious of them, so should we pour them again upon Him and set our conscience free. Therefore see well to it that you act not like perverted people, who bite and devour themselves with their sins in their heart, and run here and there with their good works or their own satisfaction, or even work themselves out of this condition by means of indulgences and become rid of their sins; which is impossible, and, alas, such a false refuge of satisfaction and pilgrimages has spread far and wide.

From "Christ's Holy Sufferings."

22

FOR IN FACT HE REMITS TO SOULS IN PURGATORY NO PENALTY
WHICH THEY WOULD HAVE HAD TO PAY IN THIS LIFE ACCORD-
ING TO THE CANONS.

Yet, though Satan has not been able to extinguish the virtue of
baptism in the case of little children, still he has had power to extinguish it in all adults; so that there is scarcely anyone nowadays who
remembers that he has been baptized, much less glories in it; so
many other ways having been found of obtaining remission of sins
and going to heaven. Occasion has been afforded to these opinions
by that perilous saying of St. Jerome, either misstated or misunderstood, in which he calls penitence the second plank of safety after
shipwreck; as if baptism were not penitence. Hence, when men
have fallen into sin, they despair of the first plank, or the ship, as
being no longer of any use, and begin to trust and depend only on
the second plank, that is, on penitence. Thence have sprung those
infinite loads of vows, religious dedications, works, satisfactions,
pilgrimages, indulgences, and systems; and from them those oceans
of books and of human questionings, opinions, and traditions,
which the whole world nowadays cannot contain. Thus this tyranny possesses the church of God in an incomparably worse form
than it ever possessed the synagogue, or any nation under heaven.

It was the duty of bishops to remove all these abuses, and to make every effort to recall Christians to the simplicity of baptism; that so they might understand their own position, and what as Christians they ought to do. But the one business of bishops at the present day is to lead the people as far as possible away from baptism and to plunge them all under the deluge of their own tyranny; and thus, as the prophet says, to make the people of Christ forget Him forever. Oh wretched men who are called by the name of bishops! They not only do nothing and know nothing that bishops ought, but they are even ignorant what they ought to know and do. They fulfill the words of Isaiah: *"His watchmen are blind; they are all ignorant.... They are shepherds that cannot understand: they all look to their own way, every one for his gain, from his quarter"* (Isaiah 56:10–11).

From "On the Babylonish Captivity of the Church."

23

IF ANY ENTIRE REMISSION OF ALL PENALTIES CAN BE GRANTED
TO ANY ONE, IT IS CERTAIN THAT IT IS GRANTED TO NONE BUT
THE MOST PERFECT, THAT IS, TO VERY FEW.

> *And for this cause he is the mediator of the new testament,
> that by means of death, for the redemption of the transgressions that were under the first testament, they which are called
> might receive the promise of eternal inheritance.*
>
> (Hebrews 9:15)

Under the old law, which provided only for formal or ritualistic pardon and restored to human fellowship, sin and transgressions remained, burdening the conscience. It—the old law—did not benefit the soul at all, inasmuch as God did not institute it to purify and safeguard the conscience, nor to bestow the Spirit. It existed merely for the purpose of outward discipline, restraint, and correction. So Paul teaches that under the Old Testament dispensation man's transgressions remained, but now Christ is our Mediator through His blood; by it our conscience is freed from sin in the sight of God, inasmuch as God promises the Spirit through the blood of Christ. All, however, do not receive Him. Only those called to be heirs eternal, the elect, receive the Spirit.

We find, then, in this excellent lesson, the comforting doctrine taught that Christ is He whom we should know as the priest and bishop of our souls; that no sin is forgiven, nor the Holy Spirit given, by reason of works or merit on our part, but alone through the blood of Christ, and that to those for whom God has ordained it.

From "Christ Our Great High Priest."

24

HENCE THE GREATER PART OF THE PEOPLE MUST NEEDS BE DECEIVED BY THIS INDISCRIMINATE AND HIGH-SOUNDING PROMISE OF RELEASE FROM PENALTIES.

The degrees of relationship in which marriage is forbidden must be altered, such as so-called spiritual relations in the third and fourth degrees; and where the pope at Rome can dispense in such matters for money, and make shameful bargains, every priest should have the power of granting the same dispensations freely for the salvation of souls. Would to God that all those things that have to be bought at Rome, for freedom from the golden noose of the canon law, might be given by any priest without payment, such as Indulgences, letters of Indulgences, letters of dispensation, mass letters, and all the other religious licenses and knaveries at Rome by which the poor people are deceived and robbed! For if the pope has the power to sell for money his golden snares, or canon nets (laws, I should say), much more has a priest the power to cancel them and to trample on them for God's sake. But if he has no such power, then the pope can have no authority to sell them in his shameful fair.

From "To the Christian Nobility of the German Nation Respecting the Reformation of the Christian Estate."

25

SUCH POWER AS THE POPE HAS OVER PURGATORY IN GENERAL, SUCH HAS EVERY BISHOP IN HIS OWN DIOCESE, AND EVERY CURATE IN HIS OWN PARISH, IN PARTICULAR.

Therefore, Leo my Father[3], beware of listening to those Sirens, who make you out to be not simply a man, but partly a God, so that you can command and require whatever you will. It will not happen so, nor will you prevail. You are the servant of servants, and, more than any other man, in a most pitiable and perilous position. Let not those men deceive you, who pretend that you are Lord of the world; who will not allow anyone to be a Christian without your authority; who babble of your having power over heaven, hell, and purgatory. These men are your enemies and are seeking your soul to destroy it, as Isaiah says: *"O my people, they which lead thee cause thee to err."* They are in error, who raise you above councils and the universal church. They are in error, who attribute to you alone the right of interpreting Scripture. All these men are seeking to set up their own impieties in the church under your name, and alas! Satan has gained much through them in the time of your predecessors.

In brief, trust not in any who exalt you, but in those who humiliate you. For this is the judgment of God: *"He hath put down*

---

3. Pope Leo X

the mighty from their seats, and exalted them of low degree" (Luke 1:52). See how unlike Christ was to His successors, though all will have it that they are His vicars. I fear that in truth very many of them have been in too serious a sense His vicars, for a vicar represents a prince who is absent. Now, if a Pontiff rules while Christ is absent and does not dwell in his heart, what else is he but a vicar of Christ? And then what is that church but a multitude without Christ? What indeed is such a vicar but Antichrist and an idol? How much more rightly did the apostles speak, who call themselves the servants of a present Christ, not the vicars of an absent one.

From "Concerning Christian Liberty."

26

THE POPE ACTS MOST RIGHTLY IN GRANTING REMISSION TO SOULS, NOT BY THE POWER OF THE KEYS (WHICH IS OF NO AVAIL IN THIS CASE) BUT BY THE WAY OF SUFFRAGE.

And I [Jesus] will give unto thee [Peter] the keys of the kingdom of heaven: and whatsoever thou shalt bind on earth shall be bound in heaven: and whatsoever thou shalt loose on earth shall be loosed in heaven. (Matthew 16:19)

It is a wickedly devised fable, and they cannot quote a single letter to confirm it, that it is for the pope alone to interpret the Scriptures or to confirm the interpretation of them: they have assumed the authority of their own selves. And though they say that this authority was given to Peter when the keys were given to him, it is plain enough that the keys were not given to Peter alone, but to the whole community. Besides, the keys were not ordained for doctrine or authority, but for sin, to bind or loose; and what they claim besides this is mere invention. But what Christ said to Peter: *"I have prayed for thee, that thy faith fail not"* (Luke 22:32), cannot relate to the pope, inasmuch as there have been many popes without faith, as they are themselves forced to acknowledge. Nor did Christ pray for Peter alone, but for all the apostles and all Christians, as He says, *"Neither pray I for these alone, but for them also which shall believe on me through their word"* (John 17:20). Is not this plain enough?

Only consider the matter. They must needs acknowledge that there are pious Christians among us that have the true faith, spirit, understanding, word, and mind of Christ; why then should we reject their word and understanding and follow a pope who has neither understanding nor Spirit? Surely this were to deny our whole faith and the Christian church. Moreover, if the article of our faith is right: I believe in the holy Christian church, the pope cannot alone be right; else we must say: I believe in the pope of Rome, and reduce the Christian church to one man, which is a devilish and damnable heresy. Besides that, we are all priests, as I have said, and have all one faith, one gospel, one sacrament; how then should we not have the power of discerning and judging what is right or wrong in matters of faith? What becomes of Paul's words: *"But he that is spiritual judgeth all things, yet he himself is judged of no man"* (1 Corinthians 2:15); and also, *"We having the same spirit of faith"* (2 Corinthians 4:13). Why then should we not perceive as well as an unbelieving pope, what agrees or disagrees with our faith?

By these and many other texts, we should gain courage and freedom, and should not let the spirit of liberty (as Paul has it) be frightened away by the inventions of the popes; we should boldly judge what they do and what they leave undone, by our own understanding of the Scriptures, and force them to follow the better understanding, and not their own. Did not Abraham in old days have to obey his Sarah, who was in stricter bondage to him than we are to any one on earth? Thus too Balaam's ass was wiser than the prophet. If God spoke by an ass against a prophet, why should He not speak by a pious man against the pope? Besides, Paul withstood Peter as being in error. (See Galatians 2:11.) Therefore it behooves every Christian to aid the faith by understanding and defending it, and by condemning all errors.

From "To the Christian Nobility of the German Nation Respecting the Reformation of the Christian Faith."

27

THEY PREACH MAN, WHO SAY THAT THE SOUL FLIES OUT OF
PURGATORY AS SOON AS THE MONEY THROWN INTO THE CHEST
RATTLES.

Now, we know ourselves to be of the same clay whereof they
are made; indeed, we perhaps have the greater call from God: yet
we cannot boast of being capable of ourselves to advise or aid men.
We cannot even originate an idea calculated to give help. And when
it comes to the knowledge of how one may stand before God and
attain to eternal life, that is truly not to be achieved by our work
or power, nor to originate in our brain. In other things, those per-
taining to this temporal life, you may glory in what you know, you
may advance the teachings of reason, you may invent ideas of your
own; for example: how to make shoes or clothes, how to govern
a household, how to manage a herd. In such things exercise your
mind to the best of your ability. Cloth or leather of this sort will
permit itself to be stretched and cut according to the good pleasure of the tailor or shoemaker. But in spiritual matters, human
reasoning certainly is not in order; other intelligence, other skill
and power, are requisite here—something to be granted by God
Himself and revealed through His Word.

What mortal has ever discovered or fathomed the truth that
the three persons in the eternal divine essence are one God; that

the second person, the Son of God, was obliged to become man, born of a virgin; and that no way of life could be opened for us, save through His crucifixion? Such truth never would have been heard nor preached, would never in all eternity have been published, learned and believed, had not God Himself revealed it.

For this season they are blind fools of first magnitude and dangerous characters who would boast of their grand performances, and think that the people are served when they preach their own fancies and inventions. It has been the practice in the church for anyone to introduce any teaching he saw fit; for example, the monks and priests have daily produced new saints, pilgrimages, special prayers, works and sacrifices in the effort to blot out sin, redeem souls from purgatory, and so on. They who make up things of this kind are not such as put their trust in God through Christ, but rather such as defy God and Christ. Into the hearts of men, where Christ alone should be, they shove the filth and write the lies of the devil. Yet they think themselves, and themselves only, qualified for all essential teaching and work, self-grown doctors that they are, saints all-powerful without the help of God and Christ.

From "Christ's Holy Sufferings."

28

It is certain that, when the money rattles in the chest, avarice and gain may be increased, but the suffrage of the church depends on the will of God alone.

What need I say further? In the whole body of the pope's canon law, there are not two lines that can instruct a pious Christian, and so many false and dangerous ones, that it were better to treat it as waste paper.

But if you object that this would give offense, and that one must first obtain the pope's dispensation, I answer that if there is any offense in it, it is the fault of the See of Rome, which has made unjust and unholy laws. It is no offense to God and the Scriptures. Even where the pope has power to grant dispensation for money by his covetous tyrannical laws, every Christian has power to grant dispensation in the same matter for the sake of Christ and the salvation of souls. For Christ has freed us from all human laws, especially when they are opposed to God and the salvation of souls, as Paul teaches. (See Galatians 5:1; 1 Corinthians 8:9–10.)

From "To the Christian Nobility of the German Nation Respecting the Reformation of the Christian Faith."

29

WHO KNOWS WHETHER ALL THE SOULS IN PURGATORY DESIRE
TO BE REDEEMED FROM IT, ACCORDING TO THE STORY TOLD OF
SAINTS SEVERINUS AND PASCHAL.

The existence of a purgatory I have never denied. I still hold
that it exists, as I have written and admitted many times, though
I have found no way of proving it incontrovertibly from Scripture
or reason. I find in Scripture that Christ, Abraham, Jacob, Moses,
Job, David, Hezekiah, and some others tasted hell in this life. This
I think was purgatory, and it seems not beyond belief that some
of the dead suffer in like manner. Tauler has much to say about
it, and, in short, I myself have come to the conclusion that there is
a purgatory, but I cannot force anybody else to come to the same
result.

There is only one thing that I have criticized, namely, the way
in which my opponents refer to purgatory passages in Scripture
that are so inapplicable that it is shameful. For example, they apply
Psalm 66:12, *"We went through fire and through water,"* though the
whole psalm sings of the sufferings of the saints, whom no one
places in purgatory. And they quote Paul in 1 Corinthians 3:13–
15 when he says of the fire of the last day that it will test the good
works, and by it some will be saved because they keep the faith,

though their work may suffer loss. They turn this fire also into a purgatory, according to their custom of twisting Scripture and making it mean whatever they want.

And similarly they have arbitrarily dragged in the passage in Matthew 12:32, in which Christ says, "*Whosoever speaketh against the Holy Ghost, it shall not be forgiven him, neither in this world, neither in the world to come.*" Christ means here that he shall never be forgiven, as Mark 3:29 explains, saying, "*He that shall blaspheme against the Holy Ghost hath never forgiveness, but is in danger of eternal damnation.*" To be sure, even St. Gregory interprets the passage in Matthew 12 to mean that some sins will be forgiven in the world to come, but Mark does not permit such an interpretation, and he counts for more than all the doctors.

I have discussed all this in order to show that no one is bound to believe more than what is based on Scripture, and those who do not believe in purgatory are not to be called heretics, if otherwise they accept Scripture in its entirety, as the Greek church does…. Especially since so much depends on this doctrine that is so important that, indeed, the papacy and the whole hierarchy are all but built upon it, and derive all their wealth and honor from it. Surely, the majority of the priests would starve to death if there were no purgatory. Well, they should not offer such vague and feeble grounds for our faith.

From *Luther's Works, Volume 32: Career of the Reformer II.*

30

NO MAN IS SURE OF THE REALITY OF HIS OWN CONTRITION,
MUCH LESS OF THE ATTAINMENT OF PLENARY REMISSION.

Although there is something in the teaching of those who
assert that contrition is to be brought about by the collection—as
they call it—and contemplation of our own sins, still theirs is a
perilous and perverse doctrine, because they do not first teach the
origin and cause of contrition, namely, the unshakeable truth of
the divine threatenings and promises, in order to call forth faith;
that so men might understand that they ought to look with much
more earnest attention to the truth of God, by which to be humbled and raised up again, than to the multitude of their own sins,
which, if they be looked at apart from the truth of God, are more
likely to renew and increase the desire for sin, than to produce contrition. I say nothing of that insurmountable chaos of labor that
they impose upon us, namely, that we are to frame a contrition
for all our sins, for this is impossible. We can know but a small
part of our sins; indeed even our good works will be found to be
sins; as it is written: *Enter not into judgment with thy servant: for in
thy sight shall no man living be justified* (Psalm 143:2). It is enough
that we sorrow for those sins that vex our conscience at the present moment, and which are easily recognized by an effort of our
memory. He who is thus disposed will, without doubt, be ready to

feel sorrow and fear on account of all his sins, and will feel sorrow and fear when in future they are revealed to him.

Beware then of trusting in thine own contrition, or attributing remission of sins to thy own sorrow. It is not because of these that God looks on thee with favor, but because of the faith with which thou hast believed His threatenings and promises, and which has wrought that sorrow in thee. Therefore, whatever good there is in penitence is due, not to the diligence with which we reckon up our sins, but to the truth of God and to our faith. All other things are works and fruits that follow of their own accord, and that do not make a man good, but are done by a man who has been made good by his faith in the truth of God. Thus it is written: "*...because he was wroth. There went up a smoke out of his nostrils...*" (Psalm 18:7–8). The terror of the threatening comes first, which devours the wicked; but faith, accepting the threatening, sends forth contrition as a cloud of smoke.

From "On the Babylonish Captivity of the Church."

31

RARE AS IS A TRUE PENITENT, SO RARE IS ONE WHO TRULY
BUYS INDULGENCES—THAT IS TO SAY, MOST RARE.

How unworthily they have treated the matter of satisfaction.
I have abundantly shown in the case of indulgences. They have
abused it notably, to the destruction of Christians in body and in
soul. In the first place, they have so taught it that the people have
not understood the real meaning of satisfaction, which is a change
of life. Furthermore, they so urge it and represent it as necessary,
that they leave no room for faith in Christ; but men's consciences
are most wretchedly tortured by scruples on this point. One runs
hither, another thither; one to Rome, another into a convent,
another to some other place; one scourges himself with rods,
another destroys his body with vigils and fasting; while all, under
one general delusion, say: Here is Christ, or there; and imagine
that the kingdom of God, which is really within us, will come with
observation. These monstrous evils we owe to you, See of Rome,
and to your homicidal laws and rites, by which you have brought
the world to such a point of ruin, that they think they can make
satisfaction to God for their sins by works, while it is only by the
faith of a contrite heart that He is satisfied.

From "On the Babylonish Captivity of the Church."

32

THOSE WHO BELIEVE THAT, THROUGH LETTERS OF PARDON, THEY ARE MADE SURE OF THEIR OWN SALVATION, WILL BE ETERNALLY DAMNED ALONG WITH THEIR TEACHERS.

Our Babylon has so utterly done away with faith as to declare with shameless front that it is not necessary in this sacrament; nay, in her anti-Christian wickedness, she pronounces it a heresy to assert the necessity of faith. What more is there that that tyranny could do, and has not done? Verily, *"By the rivers of Babylon, there we sat down, yea, we wept, when we remembered Zion. We hanged our harps upon the willows in the midst thereof"* (Psalm 137:1–2). May the Lord curse the barren willows of those rivers! Amen. The promise and faith having been blotted out and overthrown, let us see what they have substituted for them. They have divided penitence into three parts: contrition, confession, and satisfaction; but in doing this they have taken away all that was good in each of these, and have set up in each their own tyranny and caprice.

In the first place, they have so taught contrition as to make it prior to faith in the promise, and far better as not being a work of faith, but a merit; nay, they make no mention of faith. They stick fast in works and in examples taken from the Scriptures, where we read of many who obtained pardon through humility and contrition of heart, but they never think of the faith that wrought this contrition and sorrow of heart; as it is written concerning the Ninevites: *"The people of Nineveh believed God, and proclaimed a fast, and put on sackcloth"* (Jonah 3:5). These men, worse and more audacious than the Ninevites, have invented a certain "attrition," which, by the virtue of the keys (of which they are ignorant), may become contrition; and this they bestow on the wicked and unbelieving, and thus do away entirely with contrition. O unendurable wrath of God, that such things should be taught in the church of Christ! So it is that, having got rid of faith and its work, we walk heedlessly in the doctrines and opinions of men, or rather perish in them. A contrite heart is a great matter indeed, and can only proceed from an earnest faith in the divine promises and threats—a faith that, contemplating the unshakeable truth of God, makes the conscience to tremble, terrifies and bruises it, and, when it is thus contrite, raises it up again, consoles, and preserves it. Thus, the truth of the threatening is the cause of contrition, and the truth of the promise is the cause of consolation, when they are believed; and by this faith a man merits remission of sins. Therefore faith above all things ought to be taught and called forth; when faith is produced, contrition and consolation will follow of their own accord by an inevitable consequence.

From "Concerning Christian Liberty."

33

WE MUST ESPECIALLY BEWARE OF THOSE WHO SAY THAT
THESE PARDONS FROM THE POPE ARE THAT INESTIMABLE GIFT
OF GOD BY WHICH MAN IS RECONCILED TO GOD.

The papists declared also to the people, in their sermons, that
the only Mediator between God and man, our Lord and Savior
Jesus Christ, was a severe and an angry judge, who would not be
reconciled with us, except we had other advocates and intercessors
besides himself.

By this doctrine, people were seduced, and carried away to
heathenish idolatry, and took their refuge in dead saints to help
and deliver them, and made them their gods, in whom they put
more trust and confidence than in our blessed Savior Christ Jesus;
and especially, they placed the Virgin Mary, instead of her Son
Christ, for a mediatrix on the throne of grace.

Hence proceeded the pilgrimages to saints, where they sought
for pardon and remission of sins. They also sought for pardons
of the pope, of the fraternities of friars, and of other orders. And
people were taught, that they must purchase heaven by their own
good works, austerities, fasting, and so on.

And whereas prayer is the highest comfort of a Christian, yea,
his asylum, his shield and buckler against all adversities; therefore

the pope out of prayer made a naked work, a tedious babbling without spirit and truth. People praying in Latin psalters, and books that they understood not; they observed in praying, *Horae Canonicae*, or the seven times, with garlands of roses, with so many Bridget prayers, and other collects to the dead saints; and thereby wrought terror of consciences, so that people received no hope or true comfort at all. Yet, notwithstanding, they were made to believe that such prating should merit pardons and remissions of sins for the space of many thousand years.

From *Table Talk*.

34

FOR THE GRACE CONVEYED BY THESE PARDONS HAS RESPECT ONLY TO THE PENALTIES OF SACRAMENTAL SATISFACTION, WHICH ARE OF HUMAN APPOINTMENT.

Here must be added that one should abolish, or treat as of no account, or give to all churches alike, the licenses, bulls, and whatever the pope sells at his flying-ground at Rome. For if he sells or gives to Wittenberg, to Halle, to Venice, and above all to his own city of Rome, special permissions, privileges, indulgences, graces, advantages, faculties, why does he not give them to all churches alike? Is it not his duty to do all that he can for all Christians without reward, solely for God's sake, nay, even to shed his blood for them? Why then, I should like to know, does he give or sell these things to one church and not to another? Or does this accursed gold make a difference in his Holiness's eyes between Christians who all alike have baptism, gospel, faith, Christ, God, and all things? Do they wish us to be blind, when our eyes can see, to be fools, when we have reason, that we should worship this greed, knavery and delusion? He is a shepherd forsooth—so long as you have money, no further; and yet they are not ashamed to practice all this knavery right and left with their bulls. They care only for that accursed gold and for naught besides.

Therefore my advice is this: If this folly is not done away with, let all pious Christians open their eyes and not be deceived by these Romish Bulls and seals, and all their specious pretenses; let them stop at home in their own churches, and be satisfied with their baptism, gospel, faith, Christ, and God (who is everywhere the same), and let the pope continue to be a blind leader of the blind. Neither pope nor angel can give you as much as God gives you in your own parish; nay, he only leads you away from God's gifts, which you have for nothing, to his own gifts, which you must buy; giving you lead for gold, skin for meat, strings for a purse, wax for honey, words for goods, the letter for the spirit; as you can see for yourselves though you will not perceive it. If you try to ride to heaven on the pope's wax and parchment, your carriage will soon break down and you will fall into hell, not in God's name.

From "To the Christian Nobility of the German Nation Respecting the Reformation of the Christian Estate."

35

THEY PREACH NO CHRISTIAN DOCTRINE, WHO TEACH THAT
CONTRITION IS NOT NECESSARY FOR THOSE WHO BUY SOULS
OUT OF PURGATORY OR BUY CONFESSIONAL LICENSES.

Some have even proceeded to such a length in framing engines
of despair for souls, as to lay it down that all sins, the satisfaction
enjoined for which has been neglected, must be gone over afresh
in confession. What will not such men dare, men born for this
end, to bring everything ten times over into bondage? Moreover, I
should like to know how many people there are who are fully persuaded that they are in a state of salvation, and are making satisfaction for their sins, when they murmur over the prayers enjoined
by the priest with their lips alone, and meanwhile do not even
think of any amendment of life. They believe that by one moment
of contrition and confession their whole life is changed, and that
there remains merit enough over and above to make satisfaction
for their past sins. How should they know better, when they are
taught nothing better? There is not a thought here of mortification
of the flesh; the example of Christ goes for nothing; who, when
He absolved the woman taken in adultery, said to her, "Go, *and
sin no more*"; thereby laying on her the cross of mortification of the
flesh. No slight occasion has been given to these perverted ideas

by our absolving sinners before they have completed their satisfaction; whence it comes that they are more anxious about completing their satisfaction, which is a thing that lasts, than about contrition, which they think has been gone through in the act of confession.

On the contrary, absolution ought to follow the completion of satisfaction, as it did in the primitive church, whence it happened that, the work being over, they were afterwards more exercised in faith and newness of life. On this subject, however, it must suffice to have repeated so far what I have said at greater length in writing on indulgences. Let it also suffice for the present to have said this much in the whole respecting these three sacraments, which are treated of and not treated of in so many mischievous books of Sentences and of law.

From "On the Babylonish Captivity of the Church."

36

EVERY CHRISTIAN WHO FEELS TRUE COMPUNCTION HAS OF RIGHT PLENARY REMISSION OF PAIN AND GUILT, EVEN WITHOUT LETTERS OF PARDON.

If the children of Israel, when returning to God in repentance, first of all called to mind their exodus from Egypt, and in remembrance of this turned back to God, who had brought them out—a remembrance that is so often inculcated on them by Moses, and referred to by David—how much more ought we to remember our exodus from Egypt, and in remembrance of it to return to Him who brought us out through the washing of the new birth. Now this we can do most advantageously of all in the sacrament of the bread and wine. So of old these three sacraments, penitence, baptism, and the bread, were often combined in the same act of worship; and the one added strength to the other. Thus we read of a certain holy virgin who, whenever she was tempted, relied on her baptism only for defense, saying, in the briefest words: "I am a Christian." The enemy forthwith felt the efficacy of baptism, and of the faith that depended on the truth of a promising God, and fled from her.

We see then how rich a Christian, or baptized man, is; since, even if he would, he cannot lose his salvation by any sins however

great, unless he refuses to believe; for no sins whatever can condemn him, but unbelief alone. All other sins, if faith in the divine
promise made to the baptized man stands firm or is restored, are
swallowed up in a moment through that same faith; yea, through
the truth of God, because He cannot deny Himself, if thou confess
Him, and cleave believingly to His promise. Whereas contrition,
and confession of sins, and satisfaction for sins, and every effort
that can be devised by men, will desert you at your need, and will
make you more miserable than ever, if you forget this divine truth
and puff yourself up with such things as these. For whatever work
is wrought apart from faith in the truth of God is vanity and vexation of spirit.

From "On the Babylonish Captivity of the Church."

37

EVERY TRUE CHRISTIAN, WHETHER LIVING OR DEAD, HAS A
SHARE IN ALL THE BENEFITS OF CHRIST AND OF THE CHURCH,
GIVEN HIM BY GOD, EVEN WITHOUT LETTERS OF PARDON.

Preaching ought to have the object of promoting faith in Him, so that He may not only be Christ, but a Christ for you and for me, and that what is said of Him, and what He is called, may work in us. And this faith is produced and is maintained by preaching why Christ came, what He has brought us and given to us, and to what profit and advantage He is to be received. This is done, when the Christian liberty that we have from Christ Himself is rightly taught, and we are shown in what manner all we Christians are kings and priests, and how we are lords of all things, and may be confident that whatever we do in the presence of God is pleasing and acceptable to Him.

Whose heart would not rejoice in its inmost core at hearing these things? Whose heart, on receiving so great a consolation, would not become sweet with the love of Christ, a love to which it can never attain by any laws or works? Who can injure such a heart, or make it afraid? If the consciousness of sin, or the horror of death, rush in upon it, it is prepared to hope in the Lord, and is fearless of such evils, and undisturbed, until it shall look down upon its enemies. For it believes that the righteousness of Christ is its own, and that its sin is no longer its own, but that of Christ, for, on account of its faith in Christ, all its sin must needs be swallowed up from before the face of the righteousness of Christ, as I have said above. It learns too, with the apostle, to scoff at death and sin, and to say: *"O death, where is thy sting? O grave, where is thy victory? The sting of death is sin; and the strength of sin is the law. But thanks be to God, which giveth us the victory through our Lord Jesus Christ"* (1 Corinthians 15:55–57). For death is swallowed up in victory; not only the victory of Christ, but ours also; since by faith it becomes ours, and in it we too conquer.

From "Concerning Christian Liberty."

38

THE REMISSION, HOWEVER, IMPARTED BY THE POPE IS BY NO
MEANS TO BE DESPISED, SINCE IT IS, AS I HAVE SAID, A DECLA-
RATION OF THE DIVINE REMISSION.

In what darkness, unbelief, traditions, and ordinances of men
have we lived, and in how many conflicts of the conscience we
have been ensnared, confounded, and captivated under popedom,
is testified by the books of the papists, and by many people now
living. From all which snares and horrors we are now delivered and
freed by Jesus Christ and His gospel, and are called to the true
righteousness of faith; insomuch that with good and peaceable
consciences we now believe in God the Father, we trust in Him,
and have just cause to boast that we have sure and certain remission of our sins through the death of Christ Jesus, dearly bought
and purchased. Who can sufficiently extol these treasures of the
conscience, which everywhere are spread abroad, offered, and presented merely by grace? We are now conquerors of sin, of the law,
of death, and of the devil; freed and delivered from all human traditions. If we would but consider the tyranny of auricular confession, one of the least things we have escaped from, we could not
show ourselves sufficiently thankful to God for loosing us out of
that one snare. When popedom stood and flourished among us,

then every king would willingly have given ten hundred thousand guilders, a prince one hundred thousand, a nobleman one thousand, a gentleman one hundred, a citizen or countryman twenty or ten, to have been freed from that tyranny. But now seeing that such freedom is obtained for nothing, by grace, it is not much regarded, neither give we thanks to God for it.

From *Table Talk*.

39

IT IS A MOST DIFFICULT THING, EVEN FOR THE MOST LEARNED THEOLOGIANS, TO EXALT AT THE SAME TIME IN THE EYES OF THE PEOPLE THE AMPLE EFFECT OF PARDONS AND THE NECESSITY OF TRUE CONTRITION.

This ignorance[4], and this crushing of liberty, are diligently promoted by the teaching of very many blind pastors, who stir up and urge the people to a zeal for these things, praising such zeal and puffing up men with their indulgences, but never teaching faith. Now I would advise you, if you have any wish to pray, to fast, or to made foundations in churches, as they call it, to take care not to do so with the object of gaining any advantage, either temporal or eternal. You will thus wrong your faith that alone bestows all things on you, and the increase of which, either by working or by suffering, is alone to be cared for. What you give, give freely and without price, that others may prosper and have increase from you and from your goodness. Thus you will be a truly good man and a Christian. For what do you want with your goods and your works, which are done over and above for the subjection of the body, since you have abundance for yourself through your faith, in which God has given you all things?

From "Concerning Christian Liberty."

---

4. Ignorance of Christian faith.

40

TRUE CONTRITION SEEKS AND LOVES PUNISHMENT; WHILE THE AMPLENESS OF PARDONS RELAXES IT, AND CAUSES MEN TO HATE IT, OR AT LEAST GIVES OCCASION FOR THEM TO DO SO.

God is not an angry God; if He were so, we were all utterly lost and undone. God does not willingly strike mankind, except, as a just God, He be constrained thereunto; but, having no pleasure in unrighteousness and ungodliness, He must therefore suffer the punishment to go on. As I sometimes look through the fingers, when the tutor whips my son John, so it is with God; when we are unthankful and disobedient to His Word, and commandments, He suffers us, through the devil, to be soundly lashed with pestilence, famine, and such like whips; not that He is our enemy, and to destroy us, but that through such scourgings, He may call us to repentance and amendment, and so allure us to seek Him, run to Him, and call upon Him for help. Of this we have a fine example in the book of Judges, where the angel, in God's person, speaks thus: "I have stricken you so often, and ye are nothing the better for it;" (see Judges 10:11–13) and the people of Israel said: "Save thou us but now; we have sinned and done amiss: punish thou us, O Lord and do with us what thou wilt, only save us now" (see Judges 10:15). Whereupon He struck not all the people to death. In like manner did David, when he had sinned (in causing the people to be numbered, for which God punished the people with pestilence, so that 70,000 died), humble himself, saying: "Beloved, Lord, I have sinned, I have done this misdeed, and have deserved this punishment: What have these sheep done? Let thy hand be upon me, and upon my father's house," etc. Then the Lord *"repented him of the evil, and said to the angel that destroyed the people, It is enough, stay thy hand"* (2 Samuel 24:16).

From *Table Talk.*

41

APOSTOLICAL PARDONS OUGHT TO BE PROCLAIMED WITH CAU-
TION, LEST THE PEOPLE SHOULD FALSELY SUPPOSE THAT THEY
ARE PLACED BEFORE OTHER GOOD WORKS OF CHARITY.

And now let us turn to the other part, to the outward man. Here we shall give an answer to all those who, taking offense at the word of faith and at what I have asserted, say: "If faith does everything, and by itself suffices for justification, why then are good works commanded? Are we then to take our ease and do no works, content with faith?" Not so, impious men, I reply; not so. That would indeed really be the case, if we were thoroughly and completely inner and spiritual persons; but that will not happen until the last day, when the dead shall be raised. As long as we live in the flesh, we are but beginning and making advances in that which shall be completed in a future life. On this account the apostle calls that which we have in this life, the first-fruits of the Spirit. (See Romans 8:23.) In future we shall have the tenths, and the fullness of the Spirit. To this part belongs the fact I have stated before, that the Christian is the servant of all and subject to all. For in that part in which he is free, he does no works, but in that in which he is a servant, he does all works. Let us see on what principle this is so.

Although, as I have said, inwardly, and according to the spirit, a man is amply enough justified by faith, having all that he requires to have, except that this very faith and abundance ought to increase from day to day, even till the future life; still he remains in this mortal life upon earth, in which it is necessary that he should rule his own body, and have intercourse with men. Here then works begin; here he must not take his ease; here he must give heed to exercise his body by fasting, watching, labor, and other moderate discipline, so that it may be subdued to the spirit, and obey and conform itself to the inner man and faith, and not rebel against them nor hinder them, as is its nature to do if it is not kept under. For the inner man, being conformed to God, and created after the image of God through faith, rejoices and delights itself in Christ, in whom such blessings have been conferred on it; and hence has only this task before it, to serve God with joy and for naught in free love.

From "Concerning Christian Liberty."

42

CHRISTIANS SHOULD BE TAUGHT THAT IT IS NOT THE MIND OF
THE POPE THAT THE BUYING OF PARDONS IS TO BE IN ANY WAY
COMPARED TO WORKS OF MERCY.

> *Who also hath made us able ministers of the new testament;*
> *not of the letter, but of the spirit: for the letter killeth, but the*
> *spirit giveth life.* (2 Corinthians 3:6)

Now, as opposed to *"the letter,"* there is another doctrine or
message, which he terms the *"ministers of the new testament"* and *"of
the Spirit."* This doctrine does not teach what works are required
of man, for that man has already heard; but it makes known to
him what God would do for him and bestow upon him, indeed
what He has already done: He has given His Son Christ for us;
because, for our disobedience to the Law, which no man fulfils,
we were under God's wrath and condemnation. Christ made satisfaction for our sins, effected a reconciliation with God and gave
to us His own righteousness. Nothing is said in this ministration
of man's deeds; it tells rather of the works of Christ, who is unique
in that He was born of a virgin, died for sin and rose from the
dead, something no other man has been able to do. This doctrine
is revealed through none but the Holy Spirit, and none other confers the Holy Spirit. The Holy Spirit works in the hearts of them

who hear and accept the doctrine. Therefore, this ministration is termed a ministration "*of the Spirit.*"

He that can humble himself earnestly before God in Christ, has already won; otherwise, the Lord God would lose His deity, whose own work it is, that He have mercy on the poor and sorrowful, and spare them that humble themselves before Him. Were it not so, no human creature would come unto Him, or call upon Him; no man would be heard, no man saved, nor thank Him: "*The dead praise not the Lord,*" says Psalm 115:17. The devil can affright, murder, and steal; but God revives and comforts.

This little word, *God,* is, in the Scripture, a word with manifold significations, and is oftentimes understood of a thing after the nature of its operation and essence: as the devil is called a god; namely, a god of sin, of death, of despair, and damnation.

We must make due difference between this god and the upright and true God, who is a God of life, comfort, salvation, justification, and all goodness; for there are many words that bear no certain meanings, and equivocation is always the mother of error.

From *Table Talk.*

43

CHRISTIANS SHOULD BE TAUGHT THAT HE WHO GIVES TO A POOR MAN, OR LENDS TO A NEEDY MAN, DOES BETTER THAN IF HE BOUGHT PARDONS.

The Roman theologians teach that no man can know for a certainty whether he stands in the favor of God or not. This teaching forms one of the chief articles of their faith. With this teaching they tormented men's consciences, excommunicated Christ from the church, and limited the operations of the Holy Ghost.

St. Augustine observed that "every man is certain of his faith, if he has faith." This the Romanists deny. "God forbid," they exclaim piously, "that I should ever be so arrogant as to think that I stand in grace, that I am holy, or that I have the Holy Ghost." We ought to feel sure that we stand in the grace of God, not in view of our own worthiness, but through the good services of Christ. As certain as we are that Christ pleases God, so sure ought we to be that we also please God, because Christ is in us. And although we daily offend God by our sins, yet as often as we sin, God's mercy bends over us. Therefore sin cannot get us to doubt the grace of God. Our certainty is of Christ, that mighty Hero who overcame the Law, sin, death, and all evils. So long as He sits at the right hand of God to intercede for us, we have nothing to fear from the anger of God.

This inner assurance of the grace of God is accompanied by outward indications such as gladly to hear, preach, praise, and to confess Christ, to do one's duty in the station in which God has placed us, to aid the needy, and to comfort the sorrowing. These are the affidavits of the Holy Spirit testifying to our favorable standing with God.

If we could be fully persuaded that we are in the good grace of God, that our sins are forgiven, that we have the Spirit of Christ, that we are the beloved children of God, we would be ever so happy and grateful to God. But because we often feel fear and doubt we cannot come to that happy certainty.

Train your conscience to believe that God approves of you. Fight it out with doubt. Gain assurance through the Word of God. Say: "I am all right with God. I have the Holy Ghost. Christ, in whom I do believe, makes me worthy. I gladly hear, read, sing, and write of Him. I would like nothing better than that Christ's gospel be known throughout the world and that many, many be brought to faith in Him."

From *A Commentary on St. Paul's Epistle to the Galatians.*

44

BECAUSE, BY A WORK OF CHARITY, CHARITY INCREASES, AND THE MAN BECOMES BETTER; WHILE, BY MEANS OF PARDONS, HE DOES NOT BECOME BETTER, BUT ONLY FREER FROM PUNISHMENT.

There are three sorts of people: the first, the common sort, who live secure without remorse of conscience, acknowledging not their corrupt manners and natures, insensible of God's wrath, against their sins, and careless thereof. The second, those who through the law are scared, feel God's anger, and strive and wrestle with despair. The third, those that acknowledge their sins and God's merited wrath, feel themselves conceived and born in sin, and therefore deserving of perdition, but, notwithstanding, attentively hearken to the gospel, and believe that God, out of grace, for the sake of Jesus Christ, forgives sins, and so are justified before God, and afterwards show the fruits of their faith by all manner of good works.

From *Table Talk*.

45

CHRISTIANS SHOULD BE TAUGHT THAT HE WHO SEES ANY ONE
IN NEED, AND, PASSING HIM BY, GIVES MONEY FOR PARDONS,
IS NOT PURCHASING FOR HIMSELF THE INDULGENCES OF THE
POPE, BUT THE ANGER OF GOD.

As for the fraternities, together with indulgences, letters of indulgence, dispensations, masses and all the rest of such things, let it all be drowned and abolished; there is no good in it at all. If the pope has the authority to grant dispensation in the matter of eating butter and hearing masses, let him allow priests to do the same; he has no right to take the power from them. I speak also of the fraternities in which indulgences, masses, and good works are distributed. My friend, in baptism you joined a fraternity of which Christ, the angels, the saints and all Christians are members; be true to this, and satisfy it, and you will have fraternities enough. Let others make what show they wish; they are as counters compared to coins. But if there were a fraternity that subscribed money to feed the poor, or to help others in any way, this would be good, and it would have its indulgence and its deserts in heaven. But now they are good for nothing but gluttony and drunkenness.

From "To the Christian Nobility of the German Nation Respecting the Reformation of the Christian Estate."

46

CHRISTIANS SHOULD BE TAUGHT THAT, UNLESS THEY HAVE SUPERFLUOUS WEALTH, THEY ARE BOUND TO KEEP WHAT IS NECESSARY FOR THE USE OF THEIR OWN HOUSEHOLDS, AND BY NO MEANS TO LAVISH IT ON PARDONS.

It were also right to abolish annual festivals, processions, and masses for the dead, or at least to diminish their number; for we evidently see that they have become no better than a mockery, exciting the anger of God, and having no object but money-getting, eating, and drinking. How should it please God to hear the poor vigils and masses mumbled in this wretched way, neither read nor prayed? Even when they are properly read, it is not done freely for the love of God, but for the love of money and as payment of a debt. Now it is impossible that anything should please God, or win anything from Him that is not done freely, out of love for Him. Therefore, as true Christians, we ought to abolish or lessen a practice that we see is abused, and that angers God instead of appeasing Him. I should prefer, and it would be more agreeable to God's will, and far better for a foundation, church, or convent, to put all the yearly masses and vigils together into one mass, so that they would every year celebrate, on one day, a true vigil and mass with hearty sincerity, devotion, and faith, for all their benefactors.

This would be better than their thousand upon thousand masses said every year—each for a particular benefactor—without devotion and faith. My dear fellow-Christians! God cares not for much prayer, but for good prayer. Nay, He condemns long and frequent prayers, saying: *"Verily I say unto you, They have their reward"* (Matthew 6:2). But it is the greed that cannot trust God by which such practices are set up; it is afraid it will die of starvation.

From "To the Christian Nobility of the German Nation Respecting the Reformation of the Christian Estate."

47

CHRISTIANS SHOULD BE TAUGHT THAT, WHILE THEY ARE FREE
TO BUY PARDONS, THEY ARE NOT COMMANDED TO DO SO.

But Christ being come an high priest of good things to come, by a
greater and more perfect tabernacle, not made with hands.
(Hebrews 9:11)

The adornment of Aaron and his descendants, the high priests, was of a material nature, and they obtained for the people a merely formal remission of sins, performing their office in a perishable temple, or tabernacle. It was evident to men that their absolution and sanctification before the congregation was a temporal blessing confined to the present. But when Christ came upon the cross no one beheld him as he went before God in the Holy Spirit, adorned with every grace and virtue, a true High Priest. The blessings wrought by him are not temporal—a merely formal pardon—but the "blessings to come"; namely, blessings which are spiritual and eternal. Paul speaks of them as blessings to come, not that we are to await the life to come before we can have forgiveness and all the blessings of divine grace, but because now we possess them only in faith. They are as yet hidden, to be revealed in the future life. Again, the blessings we have in Christ were, from the standpoint of the Old Testament priesthood, blessings to come.

The apostle does not name the tabernacle he mentions; nor can he, so strange its nature! It exists only in the sight of God, and is ours in faith, to be revealed hereafter. It is not made with hands, like the Jewish tabernacle; in other words, not of "this building." The old tabernacle, like all buildings of its nature, necessarily was made of wood and other temporal materials created by God. God says in Isaiah 66:1–2: *"Where is the house that ye build unto me?.... For all those things hath mine hand made, and all those things have been."* But that greater tabernacle has not yet form; it is not yet finished. God is building it and he shall reveal it. Christ's words are, *"And if I go and prepare a place for you"* (John 14:3).

From "Christ Our Great High Priest."

48

CHRISTIANS SHOULD BE TAUGHT THAT THE POPE, IN GRANT-
ING PARDONS, HAS BOTH MORE NEED AND MORE DESIRE THAT
DEVOUT PRAYER SHOULD BE MADE FOR HIM, THAN THAT
MONEY SHOULD BE READILY PAID.

It is of a piece with this revolting pride, that the pope is not
satisfied with riding on horseback or in a carriage, but though he
be hale and strong, is carried by men like an idol in unheard-of
pomp. I ask you, how does this Lucifer-like pride agree with the
example of Christ, who went on foot, as did also all His apostles?
Where has there been a king who lived in such worldly pomp as he
does, who professes to be the head of all whose duty it is to despise
and flee from all worldly pomp—I mean, of all Christians? Not
that this need concern us for his own sake, but that we have good
reason to fear God's wrath, if we flatter such pride and do not show
our discontent. It is enough that the pope should be so mad and
foolish; but it is too much that we should sanction and approve it.

For what Christian heart can be pleased at seeing the pope,
when he communicates, sit still like a gracious lord and have the
sacrament handed to him on a golden reed, by a cardinal bending
on his knees before him? Just as if the holy sacrament were not
worthy that a pope, a poor miserable sinner, should stand to do

honor to his God, although all other Christians, who are much more holy than the Most Holy Father, receive it with all reverence? Could we be surprised if God visited us all with a plague, for that we suffer such dishonor to be done to God by our prelates, and approve it, becoming partners of the pope's damnable pride by our silence or flattery? It is the same when he carries the sacrament in procession. He must be carried, but the sacrament stands before him like a cup of wine on a table. In short, at Rome Christ is nothing, the pope is everything; yet they urge us and threaten us, to make us suffer and approve and honor this Antichristian scandal, contrary to God and all Christian doctrine. Now, may God so help a free Council, that it may teach the pope that he too is a man, not above God as he makes himself out to be.

From "To the Christian Nobility of the German Nation Respecting the Reformation of the Christian Estate."

49

CHRISTIANS SHOULD BE TAUGHT THAT THE POPE'S PARDONS ARE
USEFUL, IF THEY DO NOT PUT THEIR TRUST IN THEM, BUT MOST
HURTFUL, IF THROUGH THEM THEY LOSE THE FEAR OF GOD.

> *Such trust have we through Christ to God-ward: not that we
> are sufficient of ourselves to think any thing as of ourselves; but
> our sufficiency is of God.* (2 Corinthians 3:4–5)

These words are blows and thrusts for the false apostles and preachers. Paul is mortal enemy to the blockheads who make great boast, pretending to what they do not possess and to what they cannot do; who boast of having the Spirit in great measure; who are ready to counsel and aid the whole world; who pride themselves on the ability to invent something new. It is to be a surpassingly precious and heavenly thing they are to spin out of their heads, as the dreams of pope and monks have been in time past.

"We do not so," says Paul. We rely not upon ourselves or our wisdom and ability. We preach not what we have ourselves invented. But this is our boast and trust in Christ before God, that we have made of you a divine epistle; have written upon your hearts, not our thoughts, but the Word of God. We are not, however, glorifying our own power, but the works and the power of Him who has called and equipped us for such an office; from whom proceeds all you have heard and believed.

It is a glory that every preacher may claim, to be able to say with full confidence of heart: "This trust have I toward God in Christ, that what I teach and preach is truly the Word of God." Likewise, when he performs other official duties in the church—baptizes a child, absolves and comforts a sinner—it must be done in the same firm conviction that such is the command of Christ.

He who would teach and exercise authority in the church without this glory, *"It were better for him,"* as Christ says, *"that a great millstone were hanged about his neck, and that he were drowned in the depths of the sea"* (Matthew 18:6). For the devil's lies he preaches, and death is what he effects. Our papists, in time past, after much and long-continued teaching, after many inventions and works whereby they hoped to be saved, nevertheless always doubted in heart and mind whether or no they had pleased God. The teaching and works of all heretics and seditious spirits certainly do not bespeak for them trust in Christ; their own glory is the object of their teaching, and the homage and praise of the people is the goal of their desire. *"Not that we are sufficient of ourselves to think any thing as of ourselves."*

From "The Twofold Use of the Law & Gospel."

50

CHRISTIANS SHOULD BE TAUGHT THAT, IF THE POPE WERE ACQUAINTED WITH THE EXACTIONS OF THE PREACHERS OF PARDONS, HE WOULD PREFER THAT THE BASILICA OF ST. PETER SHOULD BE BURNT TO ASHES, THAN THAT IT SHOULD BE BUILT UP WITH THE SKIN, FLESH, AND BONES OF HIS SHEEP.

For, if as Christ and the apostles bid us, it is our duty to oppose the evil one, and all his works and words, and to drive him away as well as may be; how then should we look on in silence, when the pope and his followers are guilty of devilish works and words? Are we for the sake of men to allow the commandments and the truth of God to be defeated, which at our baptism we vowed to support with body and soul? Truly we should have to answer for all souls that are thus led away into error.

Therefore it must have been the arch devil himself who said, as we read in the ecclesiastical law: If the pope were so perniciously wicked, as to be dragging souls in crowds to the devil, yet he could not be deposed. This is the accursed and devilish foundation on which they build at Rome, and think that the whole world is to be allowed to go to the devil, rather than they should be opposed in their knavery. If a man were to escape punishment simply because he is above the rest, then no Christian might punish another, since

Christ has commanded each of us to esteem himself the lowest and the humblest. (See Matthew 18:4; Luke 9:48.)

Where there is sin, there remains no avoiding the punishment, as St. Gregory says: "We are all equal, but guilt makes one subject to another." Now see, how they deal with Christendom, depriving it of its freedom without any warrant from the Scriptures, out of their own wickedness, whereas God and the apostles made them subject to the secular sword; so that we must fear, that it is the work of antichrist, or a sign of his near approach.

From "To the Christian Nobility of the German Nation Respecting the Reformation of the Christian Estate."

51

CHRISTIANS SHOULD BE TAUGHT THAT, AS IT WOULD BE THE DUTY, SO IT WOULD BE THE WISH OF THE POPE, EVEN TO SELL, IF NECESSARY, THE BASILICA OF ST. PETER, AND TO GIVE OF HIS OWN MONEY TO VERY MANY OF THOSE FROM WHOM THE PREACHERS OF PARDONS EXTRACT MONEY.

All heretics have continually failed in this one point, that they do not rightly understand or know the article of justification. If we had not this article certain and clear, it were impossible we could criticize the pope's false doctrine of indulgences and other abominable errors, much less be able to overcome greater spiritual errors and vexations. If we only permit Christ to be our Savior, then we have won, for He is the only girdle that clasps the whole body together, as St. Paul excellently teaches. If we look to the spiritual birth and substance of a true Christian, we shall soon extinguish all deserts of good works; for they serve us to no use, neither to purchase sanctification, nor to deliver us from sin, death, devil, or hell.

Little children are saved only by faith, without any good works; therefore faith alone justifies. If God's power be able to effect that in one, then He is also able to accomplish it in all; for the power of the child effects it not, but the power of faith; neither is it done through the child's weakness or disability; for then that weakness would be merit of itself, or equivalent to merit. It is a mischievous thing that we miserable, sinful wretches will upbraid God, and hit Him in the teeth with our works, and think thereby to be justified before Him; but God will not allow it....

Kings and princes coin money only out of metals, but the pope coins money out of every thing—indulgences, ceremonies, dispensations, pardons; 'tis all fish comes to his net. 'Tis only baptism escapes him, for children came into the world without clothes to be stolen, or teeth to be drawn.

From "Table Talk."

52

VAIN IS THE HOPE OF SALVATION THROUGH LETTERS OF
PARDON, EVEN IF A COMMISSARY—NAY, THE POPE HIMSELF—
WERE TO PLEDGE HIS OWN SOUL FOR THEM.

The article of our justification before God is as with a son who
is born heir to all his father's goods, and comes not thereunto by
deserts, but naturally, or ordinary course. But yet, meantime, his
father admonishes him to do such and such things, and promises
him gifts to make him the more willing. As when he says to him:
if you will be good, be obedient, study diligently, then I will buy
you a fine coat; or, come to me, and I will give you an apple. In such
sort does he teach his son industry; though the whole inheritance
belongs to him of course, yet will he make him, by promises, pli-
able and willing to do what he would have done.

Even so God deals with us; He is loving unto us with friendly
and sweet words, promises us spiritual and temporal blessings,
though everlasting life is presented to you who believe in Christ,
by mere grace and mercy, gratis, without any merits, works, or
worthinesses.

And this ought we to teach in the church and in the assem-
bly of God, that God will have upright and good works, which
He has commanded, not such as we ourselves take in hand, of

our own choice and devotion, or well meaning, as the friars and priests teach in popedom, for such works are not pleasing to God, as Christ says: *"In vain do they worship me, teaching for doctrines the commandments of men"* (Matthew 15:9). We must teach of good works, yet always so that the article of justification remain pure and unfalsified. For Christ neither can nor will endure any beside Himself; He will have the bride alone; He is full of jealousy.

Should we teach: if thou believest, thou shalt be saved, whatsoever thou doest; that were stark naught; for faith is either false or feigned, or, though it be upright, yet is eclipsed, when people wittingly and willfully sin against God's command. And the Holy Spirit, which is given to the faithful, departs by reason of evil works done against the conscience, as the example of David sufficiently testifies.

From *Table Talk*.

53

They are enemies of Christ and of the pope, who, in order that pardons may be preached, condemn the word of God to utter silence in other churches.

A true Christian must hold for certain that the Word that is delivered and preached to the wicked, the dissemblers, and the ungodly, is as much God's Word, as that which is preached to godly, upright Christians, and that the true Christian church is among sinners, where good and bad are mingled together. And that the Word, whether it produce fruit or no, is, nevertheless, God's strength, which saves all that believe therein. Clearly, it will also judge the ungodly, otherwise, these might plead a good excuse before God, that they ought not to be condemned, since they had not had God's Word, and consequently could not have received it. But I teach that the preacher's words, absolution, and sacraments, are not his words or works, but God's, cleansing, absolving, binding, etc.; we are but the instruments or assistants, by whom God works. You say, it is the man that preaches, reproves, absolves, comforts, etc., though it is God that cleanses the hearts and forgives; but I say, God Himself preaches, threatens, reproves, affrights, comforts, absolves, administers the sacraments, etc. As our Savior Christ says: *"He that heareth you heareth* me" (Luke 10:16); and "...*whatsoever ye shall loose on earth shall be loosed in heaven*" (Matthew 18:18). And again: "*It is not ye that speak, but the Spirit of your Father which speaketh in you*" (Matthew 10:20).

I am sure and certain, when I go up to the pulpit to preach or read, that it is not my word I speak, but that my tongue is the pen of a ready writer, as the psalmist has it. God speaks in the prophets and men of God, as St. Peter in his epistle says: "*Holy men of God spake as they were moved by the Holy Ghost*" (2 Peter 1:21). Therefore we must not separate or part God and man, according to our natural reason and understanding. In like manner, every hearer must say: I hear not St. Paul, St. Peter, or a man speak, but God Himself.

From *Table Talk*.

54

WRONG IS DONE TO THE WORD OF GOD WHEN, IN THE SAME SERMON, AN EQUAL OR LONGER TIME IS SPENT ON PARDONS THAN ON IT.

This gospel treats of the office of the ministry, how it is constituted, what it accomplishes and how it is misused. It is indeed very necessary to know these things, for the office of preaching is second to none in Christendom. St. Paul highly esteemed this office for the reason that through it the Word of God was proclaimed that is effective to the salvation of all who believe it. He says to the Romans 1:16: *"I am not ashamed of the gospel of Christ: for it is the power of God unto salvation to every one that believeth."* We must now consider this theme, since our gospel lesson presents and includes it. It will, however, be a stench in the nostrils of the pope! But how shall I deal differently with him? The text says: *"He that entereth not by the door into the sheepfold, but climbeth up some other way, the same is a thief and a robber* [murderer]" (John 10:1).

This verse has been explained as having reference to those who climb, by their presumption, into the best church livings through favor and wealth, recommendations or their own power, not obtaining them by regular appointment and authority. And at present the most pious jurists are punishing people for running to

Rome after fees and benefices, or after ecclesiastical preferment and offices. This they call simony. The practice is truly deplorable, for much depends on being regularly called and appointed. No one should step into the office and preach from his own presumption and without a commission from those having the authority. But under present conditions, if we should wait until we received a commission to preach and to administer the sacraments, we would never perform those offices as long as we live. For the bishops in our day press into their offices by force, and those who have the power of preferment are influenced by friendship and rank. But I pass this by, and will speak of the true office, into which no one forces his way (even though his devotion urge him) without being called by others having the authority.

From "On the Office of Preaching."

55

THE MIND OF THE POPE NECESSARILY IS THAT, IF PARDONS, WHICH ARE A VERY SMALL MATTER, ARE CELEBRATED WITH SINGLE BELLS, SINGLE PROCESSIONS, AND SINGLE CEREMONIES, THE GOSPEL, WHICH IS A VERY GREAT MATTER, SHOULD BE PREACHED WITH A HUNDRED BELLS, A HUNDRED PROCESSIONS, AND A HUNDRED CEREMONIES.

O pontiffs, worthy of this venerable sacrament of orders! O princes not of the Catholic churches, but of the synagogues of Satan, yea, of very darkness! We may well cry out with Isaiah: *"Ye scornful men, that rule this people which is in Jerusalem"* (Isaiah 28:14); and with Amos: *"Woe to them that are at ease in Zion, and trust in the mountain of Samaria, which are named chief of the nations, to whom the house of Israel came!"* (Amos 6:1). O what disgrace to the church of God from these monstrosities of sacerdotalism! Where are there any bishops or priests who know the gospel, not to say preach it? Why then do they boast of their priesthood? Why do they wish to be thought holier and better and more powerful than other Christians, whom they call the laity? What unlearned person is not competent to read the Hours? Monks, hermits, and private persons, although laymen, may use the prayers of the Hours. The duty of a priest is to preach, and unless he does so, he is just as much a priest as the picture of a man is a man. Does the ordination of such babbling priests, the consecration of churches and bells, or the confirmation of children, constitute a bishop? Could not any deacon or layman do these things? It is the ministry of the word that makes a priest or a bishop.

Fly then, I counsel you; fly, young men, if you wish to live in safety; and do not seek admission to these holy rites, unless you are either willing to preach the gospel, or are able to believe that you are not made any better than the laity by this sacrament of orders. To read the Hours is nothing. To offer the mass is to receive the sacrament. What then remains in you, which is not to be found in any layman? Your tonsure and your vestments? Wretched priesthood, which consists in tonsure and vestments! Is it the oil poured on your fingers? Every Christian is anointed and sanctified in body and soul with the oil of the Holy Spirit, and formerly was allowed to handle the sacrament no less than the priests now do; although our superstition now imputes it as a great crime to the laity, if they touch even the bare cup, or the corporal; and not even a holy nun is allowed to wash the altar cloths and sacred napkins. When I see how far the sacrosanct sanctity of these orders has already gone, I expect that the time will come when the laity will not even be allowed to touch the altar, except when they offer money. I almost burst with anger when I think of the impious tyrannies of these reckless men, who mock and ruin the liberty and glory of the religion of Christ by such frivolous and puerile triflings.

From "On the Babylonish Captivity of the Church."

56

THE TREASURES OF THE CHURCH, WHENCE THE POPE GRANTS INDULGENCES, ARE NEITHER SUFFICIENTLY NAMED NOR KNOWN AMONG THE PEOPLE OF CHRIST.

This "mere motion" and lying reservation of the popes has brought about an unutterable state of things at Rome. There is a buying and a selling, a changing, exchanging, and bargaining, cheating and lying, robbing and stealing, debauchery, and villainy, and all kinds of contempt of God, that Antichrist himself could not rule worse. Venice, Antwerp, Cairo, are nothing to this fair and market at Rome, except that there things are done with some reason and justice, whilst here things are done as the devil himself could wish. And out of this ocean a like virtue overflows all the world. Is it not natural that such people should dread a reformation and a free council, and should rather embroil all kings and princes, than that their unity should bring about a council? Who would like his villainy to be exposed?...

If you bring money to this house, you can arrive at all that I have mentioned; and more than this, any sort of usury is made legitimate for money; property got by theft or robbery is here made legal. Here vows are annulled; here a monk obtains leave to quit his order; here priests can enter married life for money;

here bastards can become legitimate; and dishonor and shame may arrive at high honors; all evil repute and disgrace is knighted and ennobled; here a marriage is suffered that is in a forbidden degree, or has some other defect. Oh, what a trafficking and plundering is there! one would think that the canon laws were only so many ropes of gold, from which he must free himself who would become a Christian man. Nay, here the devil becomes a saint, and a god besides. What heaven and earth might not do, may be done by this house. Their ordinances are called compositions—compositions, forsooth! confusions rather. Oh what a poor treasury is the toll on the Rhine, compared with this holy house!

Let no one think that I say too much. It is all notorious, so that even at Rome they are forced to own that it is more terrible and worse than one can say. I have said and will say nothing of the foul dregs of private vices. I only speak of well-known public matters, and yet my words do not suffice. Bishops, priests, and especially the doctors of the universities, who are paid to do it, ought to have unanimously written and exclaimed against it. Yea, if you will turn the leaf, you will discover the truth....

Meanwhile since this devilish state of things is not only an open robbery, deceit and tyranny of the gates of hell, but also destroys Christianity, body and soul, we are bound to use all our diligence to prevent this misery and destruction of Christendom. If we wish to fight the Turks, let us begin here, where they are worst. If we justly hang thieves and behead robbers, why do we leave the greed of Rome so unpunished, who is the greatest thief and robber that has appeared or can appear on earth, and does all this in the holy name of Christ and St. Peter? Who can suffer this and be silent about it? Almost everything that he possesses has been stolen, or got by robbery, as we learn from all histories.

From "To the Christian Nobility of the German Nation Respecting the Reformation of the Christian Estate."

57

IT IS CLEAR THAT THEY ARE AT LEAST NOT TEMPORAL TREA-
SURES, FOR THESE ARE NOT SO READILY LAVISHED, BUT ONLY
ACCUMULATED, BY MANY OF THE PREACHERS.

Our contempt for these great matters justifies God's anger in
giving us over to the devil to lead us astray, to get up pilgrimages,
to found churches and chapels, to glorify the saints and to commit
other like follies, by which we are led astray from the true faith
into new false beliefs; just as he did in old time with the people
of Israel, whom he led away from the temple to countless other
places; all the while in God's name, and with the appearance of
holiness, against which all the prophets preached, suffering mar-
tyrdom for their words. But now no one preaches against it; and
probably if he did, bishops, popes, priests and monks would com-
bine to martyr him. In this way Antonius of Florence and many
others are made saints, so that their holiness may serve to produce glory and wealth, whereas otherwise they would have served
simply as good examples for the glory of God.

Even if this glorification of the saints had been good once, it is
not good now; just as many other things were good once and are
now occasion of offence and injurious, such as holidays, ecclesiastical treasures and ornaments. For it is evident that what is aimed

at in the glorification of saints is not the glory of God, nor the bettering of Christendom, but money and fame alone; one church wishes to have an advantage over another, and would be sorry to see another church enjoying the same advantages. In this way they have in these latter days abused the goods of the church so as to gain the goods of the world; so that everything, and even God Himself, must serve their avarice. Moreover these privileges cause nothing but dissensions and worldly pride; one church being different from the rest, they despise or magnify one another, whereas all goods that are of God should be common to all, and should serve to produce unity. This, too, is why they please the pope, who would be sorry to see all Christians equal and at one with one another.

From "To the Christian Nobility of the German Nation Respecting the Reformation of the Christian Estate."

58

NOR ARE THEY THE MERITS OF CHRIST AND OF THE SAINTS, FOR THESE, INDEPENDENTLY OF THE POPE, ARE ALWAYS WORKING GRACE TO THE INNER MAN, AND THE CROSS, DEATH, AND HELL TO THE OUTER MAN.

We are baptized and made Christians, not to the end that we may have great honor, or renown of righteousness, or earthly dominion, power, and possessions. Notwithstanding we do have these because they are requisite to our physical life, yet we are to regard them as mere filth, wherewith we minister to our bodily welfare as best we can for the benefit of posterity. We Christians, however, are expectantly to await the coming of the Savior. His coming will not be to our injury or shame as it may be in the case of others. He comes for the salvation of our unprofitable, impotent bodies. Wretchedly worthless as they are in this life, they are much more unprofitable when lifeless and perishing in the earth.

But, however miserable, powerless, and contemptible in life and death, Christ will at His coming render our bodies beautiful, pure, shining, and worthy of honor, until they correspond to His own immortal, glorious body. Not like it as it hung on the cross or lay in the grave, bloodstained, livid, and disgraced; but as it is now, glorified at the Father's right hand. We need not, then, be alarmed at the necessity of laying aside our earthly bodies; at being despoiled of the honor, righteousness, and life adhering in them, to deliver it to the devouring power of death and the grave—something well calculated to terrify the enemies of Christ: but we may joyfully hope for and await His speedy coming to deliver us from this miserable, filthy pollution.

> *According to the working whereby he is able even to subdue all things unto himself.* (Philippians 3:21)

From "Enemies of the Cross of Christ."

59

St. Lawrence said that the treasures of the church are the poor of the church, but he spoke according to the use of the word in his time.

My advice is that the Sees of the protestant bishops be permitted to remain, for the profit and use of poor students and schools; and when a bishop, dean, or provost, cannot, or will not preach himself, then he shall, at his own charge, maintain other students and scholars, and permit them to study and preach. But when potentates and princes take spiritual livings to themselves, and will famish poor students and scholars, then the parishes of necessity must be wasted, as is the case already, for we can get neither ministers nor deacons. The pope, although he be our mortal enemy, must maintain us, yet against his will, and for which he has no thanks.

These times are evil, in that the church is so spoiled and robbed by the princes and potentates; they give nothing, but take and steal. In former times they gave liberally to her, now they rob her. The church is more torn and tattered than a beggar's cloak; nothing is added to the stipends of the poor servants of the church. They who bestow them to the right use are persecuted, it going with them as with St. Lawrence, who, against the emperor's command, divided the church livings among the poor.

From *Table Talk*.

60

WE ARE NOT SPEAKING RASHLY WHEN WE SAY THAT THE
KEYS OF THE CHURCH, BESTOWED THROUGH THE MERITS OF
CHRIST, ARE THAT TREASURE.

Since then this faith can reign only in the inward man, as it
is said: *"With the heart man believeth unto righteousness"* (Romans
10:10); and since it alone justifies, it is evident that by no outward
work or labor can the inward man be at all justified, made free,
and saved; and that no works whatever have any relation to him.
And so, on the other hand, it is solely by impiety and incredulity of
heart that he becomes guilty, and a slave of sin, deserving condemnation; not by any outward sin or work. Therefore the first care of
every Christian ought to be, to lay aside all reliance on works, and
strengthen his faith alone more and more, and by it grow in the
knowledge, not of works, but of Christ Jesus, who has suffered and
risen again for him; as Peter teaches, when he makes no other work
to be a Christian one. Thus Christ, when the Jews asked Him what
they should do that they might work the works of God, rejected
the multitude of works, with which He saw that they were puffed
up, and commanded them one thing only, saying: *"This is the work
of God, that ye believe on him whom he hath sent"* (John 6:29).

Hence a right faith in Christ is an incomparable treasure, car-
rying with it universal salvation, and preserving from all evil, as it

is said: *"He that believeth and is baptized shall be saved; but he that believeth not shall be damned"* (Mark 16:16). Isaiah, looking to this treasure, predicted: *"The consumption decreed shall overflow with righteousness. For the Lord GOD of hosts shall make a consumption, even determined, in the midst of all the land"* (Isaiah 10:22–23). As if he said, "Faith, which is the brief and complete fulfilling of the law, will fill those who believe with such righteousness, that they will need nothing else for justification." Thus too Paul says: *"For with the heart man believeth unto righteousness"* (Romans 10:10).

From "Concerning Christian Liberty."

61

FOR IT IS CLEAR THAT THE POWER OF THE POPE IS ALONE SUF-
FICIENT FOR THE REMISSION OF PENALTIES AND OF RESERVED
CASES.

God promised of old, in Joel 2:28 and other passages, to give
the Spirit through the new message, the gospel. And He has veri-
fied His promise by public manifestations in connection with the
preaching of that gospel, as on the day of Pentecost and again later.
When the apostles, Peter and others, began to preach, the Holy
Spirit descended visibly from heaven upon their hearts. (See Acts
8:17; 10:44.) Up to that time, throughout the period the Law was
preached, no one had heard or seen such manifestation. The fact
could not but be grasped that this was a vastly different message
from that of the Law when such mighty results followed in its
train. And yet its substance was no more than what Paul declared:
*"Through this man is preached unto you the forgiveness of sins: and by
him all that believe are justified from all things, from which ye could not
be justified by the law of Moses"* (Acts 13:38–39).

In this teaching you see no more the empty letters, the value-
less husks or shells of the Law, which unceasingly enjoins, "This
thou shalt do and observe," and ever in vain. You see instead the
true kernel and power which confers Christ and the fullness of

His Spirit. In consequence, men heartily believe the message of the gospel and enjoy its riches. They are accounted as having fulfilled the Ten Commandments. John says: *"Of his fullness we all received, and grace for grace. For the law was given through Moses, but grace and truth came by Jesus Christ"* (John 1:16–17). John's thought is: The Law has indeed been given by Moses, but what avails that fact? To be sure, it is a noble doctrine and portrays a beautiful and instructive picture of man's duty to God and all mankind; it is really excellent as to the letter. Yet it remains empty; it does not enter into the heart. Therefore it is called "law," nor can it become aught else, so long as nothing more is given.

From "The Twofold Use of the Law & Gospel."

62

THE TRUE TREASURE OF THE CHURCH IS THE HOLY GOSPEL OF THE GLORY AND GRACE OF GOD.

Let this be a fixed rule for you: Whatever has to be bought of the pope is neither good, nor of God. For whatever comes from God is not only given freely, but all the world is punished and condemned for not accepting it freely. So is it with the gospel and the works of God. We have deserved to be led into these errors, because we have despised God's holy Word and the grace of baptism, as St. Paul says: *"And for this cause God shall send them strong delusion, that they should believe a lie: that they all might be damned who believed not the truth, but had pleasure in unrighteousness"* (2 Thessalonians 2:11–12).

From "To the Christian Nobility of the German Nation Respecting the Reformation of the Christian Estate."

63

THIS TREASURE, HOWEVER, IS DESERVEDLY MOST HATEFUL, BECAUSE IT MAKES THE FIRST TO BE LAST.

If we took away ninety-nine parts of the pope's court and only left one hundredth, it would still be large enough to answer questions on matters of belief. Now there is such a swarm of vermin at Rome, all called Papal, that Babylon itself never saw the like. There are more than three thousand Papal secretaries alone; but who shall count the other office-bearers, since there are so many offices that we can scarcely count them, and all waiting for German benefices, as wolves wait for a flock of sheep? I think Germany now pays more to the pope, than it formerly paid the Emperors; nay, some think more than three hundred thousand guilders are sent from Germany to Rome every year, for nothing whatever; and in return we are scoffed at and put to shame. Do we still wonder why princes, noblemen, cities, foundations, convents and people are poor? We should rather wonder that we have anything left to eat.

Now that we have got well into our game, let us pause awhile and show that the Germans are not such fools, as not to perceive or understand this Romish trickery. I do not here complain, that God's commandments and Christian justice are despised at Rome; for the state of things in Christendom, especially at Rome, is too bad for us to complain of such high matters. Nor do I even complain that no account is taken of natural or secular justice and reason. The mischief lies still deeper. I complain that they do not observe their own fabricated canon law, though this is in itself rather mere tyranny, avarice and worldly pomp, than a law.

From "To the Christian Nobility of the German Nation Respecting the Reformation of the Christian Estate."

64

WHILE THE TREASURE OF INDULGENCES IS DESERVEDLY MOST
ACCEPTABLE, BECAUSE IT MAKES THE LAST TO BE FIRST.

It was not principalities, powers, and dominions that Christ
instituted in His church, but a ministry, as we learn from the
words of the apostle: *"Let a man so account of us, as of the ministers
of Christ, and stewards of the mysteries of God"* (1 Corinthians 4:1).
When Christ said: *"He that believeth and is baptized shall be saved"*
(Mark 16:16), He meant to call forth faith on the part of those
seeking baptism; so that, on the strength of this word of promise, a man might be sure that, if he believed and were baptized, he
would obtain salvation. No sort of power is here bestowed on His
servants, but only the ministry of baptism is committed to them.
In the same way, when Christ says: *"Whatsoever ye shall bind..."*
(Matthew 18:18), etc., He means to call forth the faith of the penitent, so that, on the strength of this word of promise, he may be
sure that, if he believes and is absolved, he will be truly absolved in
heaven. Evidently nothing is said here of power, but it is the ministry of absolution that is spoken of. It is strange enough that these
blind and arrogant men have not arrogated to themselves some
tyrannical power from the terms of the baptismal promise. If not,
why have they presumed to do so from the promise connected with
penitence? In both cases there is an equal ministry, a like promise,

and the same character in the sacrament; and it cannot be denied that, if we do not owe baptism to Peter alone, it is a piece of impious tyranny to claim the power of the keys for the pope alone.

Thus also when Christ says: "Take, eat, this is my body which is given for you; this is the cup in my blood" (see 1 Corinthians 11:24–25), He means to call forth faith in those who eat, that their conscience may be strengthened by faith in these words, and that they may feel sure that, when they believe eat, they receive remission of sins. There is nothing here that speaks of power, but only of a ministry. The promise of baptism has remained with us, at least in the case of infants, but the promise of the bread and the cup has been destroyed, or brought into servitude to avarice, and faith has been turned into a work and a testament into a sacrifice. Thus also the promise of penance has been perverted into a most violent tyranny, and into the establishment of a dominion that is more than temporal.

From "On the Babylonish Captivity of the Church."

65

HENCE THE TREASURES OF THE GOSPEL ARE NETS, WHERE-
WITH OF OLD THEY FISHED FOR THE MEN OF RICHES.

So many misuse the gospel and few lay hold of it aright. True it is unpleasant to preach to those who treat the gospel so shamefully and even oppose it. For preaching is to become so universal that the gospel is to be proclaimed to all creatures, as Christ says in Mark 16:15: *"Preach the gospel to every creature"*; and Psalm 19:4: *"Their line is gone out through all the earth, and their words to the end of the world."* What business is it of mine that many do not esteem it? It must be that many are called but few are chosen. For the sake of the good ground that brings forth fruit with patience, the seed must also fall fruitless by the wayside, on the rock and among the thorns; inasmuch as we are assured that the Word of God does not go forth without bearing some fruit, but it always finds also good ground; as Christ says, some seed of the sower falls also into good ground, and not only by the wayside, among the thorns and on stony ground. For wherever the gospel goes you will find Christians. *"So shall my word be that goeth forth out of my mouth: it shall not return unto me void, but it shall accomplish that which I please, and it shall prosper in the thing whereto I sent it"* (Isaiah 55:11).

From "The Parable of the Sower."

The treasures of indulgences are nets, wherewith they now fish for the riches of men.

Blessed be the God and Father of our Lord Jesus Christ, who according to the riches of His mercy has at least preserved this one sacrament[5] in His church uninjured and uncontaminated by the devices of men, and has made it free to all nations and to men of every class. He has not suffered it to be overwhelmed with the foul and impious monstrosities of avarice and superstition; doubtless having this purpose, that He would have little children, incapable of avarice and superstition, to be initiated into this sacrament, and to be sanctified by perfectly simple faith in His word. To such, even at the present day, baptism is of the highest advantage. If this sacrament had been intended to be given to adults and those of full age, it seems as if it could have hardly preserved its efficacy and its glory, in the presence of that tyranny of avarice and superstition which has supplanted all divine ordinances among us. In this case too, no doubt, fleshly wisdom would have invented its preparations, its worthinesses, its reservations, its restrictions, and other like nets for catching money; so that the water of baptism would be sold no cheaper than parchments are now.

From "On the Babylonish Captivity of the Church."

---

5. baptism

67

THOSE INDULGENCES, WHICH THE PREACHERS LOUDLY PRO-
CLAIM TO BE THE GREATEST GRACES, ARE SEEN TO BE TRULY
SUCH AS REGARDS THE PROMOTION OF GAIN.

The country chapels and churches must be destroyed, such
as those to which the new pilgrimages have been set on foot,
Wilsnacht, Sternberg, Treves, the Grimmenthal, and now
Ratisbon, and many others. Oh what a reckoning there will be for
those bishops that allow these inventions of the devil and make a
profit out of them! They should be the first to stop it; they think
that it is a godly, holy thing, and do not see that the devil does this
to strengthen covetousness, to teach false beliefs, to weaken parish
churches, to increase drunkenness and debauchery, to waste
money and labor, and simply to lead the poor people by the nose.
If they had only studied the Scriptures as much as their accursed
canon law, they would know well how to deal with the matter.

The miracles performed there prove nothing, for the evil one
can also show wonders, as Christ has taught us. (See Matthew
24:24.) If they took up the matter earnestly, and forbade such
doings, the miracles would soon cease; or if they were done by
God, they would not be prevented by their commands. And if
there were nothing else to prove that these are not works of God, it
would be enough that people go about turbulently and irrationally

like herds of cattle, which could not possibly come from God. God has not commanded it; there is no obedience, and no merit in it; and therefore it should be vigorously interfered with and the people warned against it. For what is not commanded by God and goes beyond God's commandments is surely the devil's own work. In this way also the parish churches suffer, in that they are less venerated. In fine, these pilgrimages are signs of great want of faith in the people; for if they truly believed, they would find all things in their own churches, where they are commanded to go.

But what is the use of my speaking? Every man thinks only how he may get up such a pilgrimage in his own district, not caring whether the people believes and lives rightly. The rulers are like the people—blind leaders of the blind. Where pilgrimages are a failure, they begin to glorify their saints; not to honor the saints, who are sufficiently honored without them, but to cause a concourse, and to bring in money. Then pope and bishops help them; it rains indulgences, and every one can afford to buy them; but what God has commanded no one cares for; no one runs after it, no one can afford any money for it. Alas for our blindness, that we not only suffer the devil to have his way with his phantoms, but support him! I wish one would leave the good saints alone and not lead the poor people astray. What spirit gave the pope authority to "glorify" the saints? Who tells him whether they are holy, or not holy? Are there not enough sins on earth, as it is, but we must tempt God, interfere in His judgment, and make moneybags of His saints? Therefore my advice is to let the saints glorify themselves; or rather, God alone should glorify them, and every man should keep to his own parish, where he will profit more than in all these shrines, even if they were all put together into one shrine. Here a man finds baptism, the sacrament, preaching, and his neighbor, and these are more than all the saints in heaven, for it is by God's Word and sacrament that they have all been hallowed.

From "To the Christian Nobility of the German Nation Respecting the Reformation of the Christian Estate."

68

YET THEY ARE IN REALITY IN NO DEGREE TO BE COMPARED TO
THE GRACE OF GOD AND THE PIETY OF THE CROSS.

The temporal possessions of the church should not be too strictly claimed; but since we are Christians and bound to help one another, we have the right to give them these things for the sake of unity, and to let them keep them, before God and the world; for Christ says: *"Where two or three are gathered together in my name, there am I in the midst of them"* (Matthew 18:20). Would to God, we helped on both sides to bring about this unity, giving our hands one to the other in brotherly humility, not insisting on our authority or our rights! Love is more, and more necessary than the Papacy at Rome; the Papacy can exist without love, and love can exist without the Papacy. I hope I have done my best for this end. If the pope or his followers hinder this good work, they will have to give an account of their actions, for having, against the love of God, sought their own advantage more than their neighbors'. The pope should abandon his Papacy, all his possessions and honors, if he could save a soul by so doing. But he would rather see the world go to ruin than give up a hair's breadth of the power he has usurped; and yet he would be our most holy father! Herewith am I at least excused.

From "To the Christian Nobility of the German Nation Respecting the
Reformation of the Christian Estate."

69

BISHOPS AND CURATES ARE BOUND TO RECEIVE THE COMMIS-
SARIES OF APOSTOLICAL PARDONS WITH ALL REVERENCE.

We see then that just as those that we call spiritual, or priests,
bishops or popes, do not differ from other Christians in any other
or higher degree, but in that they are to be concerned with the
Word of God, and the sacraments—that being their work and
office—in the same way the temporal authorities hold the sword
and the rod in their hands to punish the wicked and to protect the
good. A cobbler, a smith, a peasant, every man has the office and
function of his calling, and yet all alike are consecrated priests and
bishops, and every man in his office must be useful and beneficial
to the rest, that so many kinds of work may all be united into one
community: just as the members of the body all serve one another.

Now see, what a Christian doctrine is this: that the temporal authority is not above the clergy, and may not punish it. This
is, as if one were to say, the hand may not help, though the eye
is in grievous suffering. Is it not unnatural, not to say unchris-
tian, that one member may not help another, or guard it against
harm? Nay, the nobler the member, the more the rest are bound
to help it. Therefore I say: forasmuch as the temporal power
has been ordained by God for the punishment of the bad, and

the protection of the good, therefore we must let it do its duty throughout the whole Christian body, without respect of persons: whether it strike popes, bishops, priests, monks, or nuns. If it were sufficient reason for fettering the temporal power that it is inferior among the offices of Christianity to the offices of priest or confessor, or to the spiritual estate—if this were so, then we ought to restrain tailors, cobblers, masons, carpenters, cooks, servants, peasants, and all secular workmen, from providing the pope, or bishops, priests and monks, with shoes, clothes, houses or victuals, or from paying them tithes. But if these laymen are allowed to do their work without restraint, what do the Romanist scribes mean by their laws? They mean that they withdraw themselves from the operation of temporal Christian power, simply in order that they may be free to do evil, and thus fulfill what St. Peter said: *"There shall be false teachers among you.... And through covetousness shall they with feigned words make merchandise of you"* (2 Peter 2:1, 3).

Therefore the temporal Christian power must exercise its office without let or hindrance, without considering whom it may strike, whether pope, or bishop, or priest: whoever is guilty let him suffer for it. Whatever the ecclesiastical law says in opposition to this, is merely the invention of Romanist arrogance. For this is what St. Paul says to all Christians: *"Let every soul* [I presume including the popes—Luther] *be subject unto the higher powers.... For he beareth not the sword in vain: for he is the minister of God, a revenger to execute wrath upon him that doeth evil"* (Romans 13:1, 4). Also St. Peter: *"Submit yourselves to every ordinance of man for the Lord's sake.... For so is the will of God"* (1 Peter 2:13, 15). He has also said, that men would come, who should despise government (see 2 Peter 2); as has come to pass through ecclesiastical law.

From "To the Christian Nobility of the German Nation Respecting the Reformation of the Christian Estate."

70

BUT THEY ARE STILL MORE BOUND TO SEE TO IT WITH ALL
THEIR EYES, AND TAKE HEED WITH ALL THEIR EARS, THAT
THESE MEN DO NOT PREACH THEIR OWN DREAMS IN PLACE OF
THE POPE'S COMMISSION.

What has happened in this very year? The bishop of Strasburg, wishing to regulate his See in a proper way and reform it in the matter of divine service, published some divine and Christian ordinances for that purpose. But our worthy pope and the holy Chair at Rome overturns altogether this holy and spiritual order on the accusation of the priests. This is what they call being the shepherd of Christ's sheep—supporting priests against their own bishops, and protecting their disobedience by divine decrees. Antichrist, I hope, will not insult God in this open way. There you have the pope, as you have chosen to have him, and why? Why, because if the church were to be reformed, many things would have to be destroyed, and possibly Rome among them. Therefore it is better to prevent priests from being at one with each other; they should rather, as they have done hitherto, sow discord among kings and princes, flood the world with Christian blood, lest Christian unity should trouble the holy Roman See with reforms.

So far we have seen what they do with the livings that fall vacant. Now there are not enough vacancies for this delicate greed;

therefore it has also taken prudent account of the benefices that are still held by their incumbents, so that they may become vacant, though they are in fact not vacant.

From "To the Christian Nobility of the German Nation Respecting the Reformation of the Christian Estate."

71

He who speaks against the truth of apostolical pardons, let him be anathema and accursed.

Let us consider this as the first virtue of faith; and let us look also to the second. This also is an office of faith, that it honors with the utmost veneration and the highest reputation him in whom it believes, inasmuch as it holds him to be truthful and worthy of belief. For there is no honor like that reputation of truth and righteousness, with which we honor him, in whom we believe. What higher credit can we attribute to any one than truth and righteousness, and absolute goodness? On the other hand, it is the greatest insult to brand anyone with the reputation of falsehood and unrighteousness, or to suspect him of these, as we do when we disbelieve him.

Thus the soul, in firmly believing the promises of God, holds Him to be true and righteous; and it can attribute to God no higher glory than the credit of being so. The highest worship of God is to ascribe to Him truth, righteousness, and whatever qualities we must ascribe to one in whom we believe. In doing this the soul shows itself prepared to do His whole will; in doing this it hallows His name, and gives itself up to be dealt with as it may please God. For it cleaves to His promises, and never doubts that

He is true, just, and wise, and will do, dispose, and provide for all things in the best way. Is not such a soul, in this its faith, most obedient to God in all things? What commandment does there remain which has not been amply fulfilled by such an obedience? What fulfillment can be more full than universal obedience? Now this is not accomplished by works, but by faith alone.

On the other hand, what greater rebellion, impiety, or insult to God can there be, than not to believe His promises? What else is this, than either to make God a liar, or to doubt His truth—that is, to attribute truth to ourselves, but to God falsehood and levity? In doing this, is not a man denying God and setting himself up as an idol in his own heart? What then can works, done in such a state of impiety, profit us, were they even angelic or apostolic works? Rightly hath God shut up all—not in wrath nor in lust—but in unbelief; in order that those who pretend that they are fulfilling the law by works of purity and benevolence (which are social and human virtues), may not presume that they will therefore be saved; but, being included in the sin of unbelief, may either seek mercy, or be justly condemned.

But when God sees that truth is ascribed to Him, and that in the faith of our hearts He is honored with all the honor of which He is worthy; then in return He honors us on account of that faith; attributing to us truth and righteousness. For faith produces truth and righteousness, in rendering to God what is His; and therefore in return God gives glory to our righteousness. It is a true and righteous thing, that God is true and righteous; and to confess this, and ascribe these attributes to Him, is to be ourselves true and righteous. Thus He says: *"Them that honour me I will honour, and they that despise me shall be lightly esteemed"* (1 Samuel 2:30). And so Paul says that Abraham's faith was imputed to him for righteousness, because by it he gave glory to God; and that to us also, for the same reason, it shall be reputed for righteousness, if we believe. (See Romans 4.)

From "Concerning Christian Liberty."

72

BUT HE, ON THE OTHER HAND, WHO EXERTS HIMSELF AGAINST THE WANTONNESS AND LICENSE OF SPEECH OF THE PREACHERS OF PARDONS, LET HIM BE BLESSED.

I do not hesitate to say that whosoever voluntarily confesses his sins privately, in the presence of any brother, or, when told of his faults, asks pardon and amends his life, is absolved from his secret sins, since Christ has manifestly bestowed the power of absolution on every believer in Him, with whatever violence the pontiffs may rage against this truth. Add also this little argument, that, if any reservation of hidden sins were valid, and there could be no salvation unless they were remitted, the greatest hindrance to salvation would lie in those things which I have mentioned above—even those good works and idolatries that we are taught at the present day by the pontiffs. While, if these most weighty matters are not a hindrance, with how much less reason are those lighter offenses so foolishly reserved! It is by the ignorance and blindness of the pastors that these portents are wrought in the church. Wherefore I would warn these princes of Babylon and bishops of Beth-aven to abstain from reserving cases of any kind whatever, but to allow the freest permission to hear confessions of secret sins to all brethren and sisters; so that the sinner may reveal his sin to whom he will, with the object of seeking pardon and consolation, that is, the word of Christ uttered by the mouth of his neighbor. They effect nothing by their rash presumption, but to ensnare needlessly the consciences of the weak, to establish their own wicked tyranny, and to feed their own avarice on the sins and perdition of their brethren. Thus they stain their hands with the blood of souls, and children are devoured by their parents, and Ephraim devours Judah, and Syria Israel, as Isaiah says.

From "On the Babylonish Captivity of the Church."

73

As the pope justly thunders against those who use any kind of contrivance to the injury of the traffic in pardons.

After the persecution of the church ceased, the popes aimed at the government, out of covetousness and ambition. The first was Hildebrand, or rather Hellbrand; they affrighted the people with their excommunication, which was so fearful a thing, that it descended upon the children, nay, fell upon servants. On the other hand, the pope seeking the goodwill of the people, granted and sold the remission of sins, were they never so heavy. Had one ravished the Virgin Mary, or crucified Christ anew, the pope would, for money, have pardoned him. This power and domination of the pope's, God has brought to confusion and destruction by my pen; for God, out of nothing, can make all things, and of the least means produce the greatest results....

When Satan says in thy heart: "God will not pardon your sins, nor be gracious to you," I pray, how will you then, as a poor sinner, raise up and comfort yourself, especially when other signs of God's wrath beat on your, as sickness, poverty, etc. And when your heart begins to preach and say: behold, here you lie in sickness; you are poor and forsaken of every one; why, you must turn yourself to the other side, and say: "Well, let it outwardly seem as it will, yea, though my own heart felt infinitely more sorrow, yet I know for certain, that I am united and made one with my Lord and Savior Christ; I have His word to assure me of the same, which can neither fail nor deceive me, for God is true, and performs what He promises."

The devil often casts this into my breast: "How, if your doctrine be false and erroneous, wherewith the pope, the mass, friars and nuns are thus dejected and startled?" at which the sour sweat has drizzled from me. But at last, when I saw he would not leave, I gave him this answer: "Avoid, Satan; address yourself to my God, and talk with Him about it, for the doctrine is not mine, but His; He has commanded me to hearken unto this Christ."

From *Table Talk*.

74

MUCH MORE IS IT HIS INTENTION TO THUNDER AGAINST
THOSE WHO, UNDER THE PRETEXT OF PARDONS, USE CONTRIV-
ANCES TO THE INJURY OF HOLY CHARITY AND OF TRUTH.

Whether I will or not, I am compelled to become more learned
day by day, since so many great masters vie with each other in
urging me on and giving me practice. I wrote about indulgences
two years ago, but now I extremely regret having published that
book. At that time I was still involved in a great and superstitious
respect for the tyranny of Rome, which led me to judge that indulgences were not to be totally rejected, seeing them, as I did, to be
approved by so general a consent among men. And no wonder, for
at that time it was I alone who was rolling this stone. Afterward,
however, with the kind aid of Sylvester and the friars, who supported indulgences so strenuously, I perceived that they were
nothing but mere impostures of the flatterers of Rome, whereby
to make away with the faith of God and the money of men. And
I wish I could prevail upon the booksellers, and persuade all who
have read them, to burn the whole of my writings on indulgences,
and in place of all I have written about them to adopt this proposition: Indulgences are wicked devices of the flatterers of Rome.

After this, Eccius and Emser, with their fellow conspirators,
began to instruct me concerning the primacy of the pope. Here

too, not to be ungrateful to such learned men, I must confess that their works helped me on greatly; for, while I had denied that the Papacy had any divine right, I still admitted that it had a human right. But after hearing and reading the super-subtle subtleties of those coxcombs, by which they so ingeniously set up their idol—my mind being not entirely unteachable in such matters—I now know and am sure that the Papacy is the kingdom of Babylon, and the power of Nimrod the mighty hunter. Here moreover, that all may go prosperously with my friends, I entreat the booksellers, and entreat my readers, to burn all that I have published on this subject, and to hold to the following proposition: The Papacy is the mighty hunting of the bishop of Rome.

From "On the Babylonish Captivity of the Church."

75

To think that papal pardons have such power that they could absolve a man even if—by an impossibility—he had violated the Mother of God, is madness.

Although I exhort men to endure the violence of these reservers, even as Christ bids us to endure all the tyrannical conduct of men, and teaches us to obey such extortioners; still, I neither admit nor believe that they have any right of reservation. By no jot or tittle can they prove this; while I can prove the contrary. In the first place, if, in speaking of public offenses, Christ says that we have gained our brother, if he hears us when told of his fault, and that he is not to be brought before the church, unless he has refused to hear us, and that offenses may thus be set right between brethren; how much more true will it be concerning private offenses, that the sin is taken away, when brother has voluntarily confessed it to brother, so that he need not bring it before the church, that is, before a prelate or priest, as these men say in their foolish interpretation. In support of my opinion we have again the authority of Christ, when He says in the same passage: "*Whatsoever ye shall bind on earth shall be bound in heaven; and whatsoever ye shall loose on earth shall be loosed in heaven*" (Matthew 18:18). This saying is addressed to all Christians and to every Christian. Once more

He says to the same effect: *"Again I say unto you, that if two of you shall agree on earth as touching anything that they shall ask, it shall be done for them of my Father which is in heaven"* (Matthew 18:19). Now a brother, laying open his secret sins to a brother and seeking pardon, certainly agrees on earth with that brother in the truth, which is Christ. In confirmation of what he had said before, Christ says still more clearly in the same passage: *"Where two or three are gathered together in my name, there am I in the midst of them"* (verse 20).

From "On the Babylonish Captivity of the Church."

76

WE AFFIRM ON THE CONTRARY THAT PAPAL PARDONS CANNOT TAKE AWAY EVEN THE LEAST OF VENIAL SINS, AS REGARDS ITS GUILT.

> *Brethren, be followers together of me, and mark them which walk so as ye have us for an ensample. (For many walk, of whom I have told you often, and now tell you even weeping, that they are the enemies of the cross of Christ: whose end is destruction, whose God is their belly, and whose glory is in their shame, who mind earthly things.) For our conversation is in heaven; from whence also we look for the Saviour, the Lord Jesus Christ: who shall change our vile body, that it may be fashioned like unto his glorious body, according to the working whereby he is able even to subdue all things unto himself.*
> (Philippians 3:17–21)

Meantime, while we walk in the faith of His righteousness, He has patience with the poor, frail righteousness of this earthly life, which otherwise is but filth in His sight. He honors our human holiness by supporting and protecting it during the time we live on earth; just as we honor our corrupt, filthy bodies, adorning them with beautiful, costly garments and golden ornaments, and reposing them on cushions and beds of luxury. Though but stench and filth encased in flesh, they are honored above everything else on earth. For their sake are all things performed—the ordering and ruling, building, and laboring; and God himself permits sun and moon to shine that they may receive light and heat, and everything to grow on earth for their benefit. What is the human body but a beautiful pyx containing that filthy, repulsive object of reverence, the digestive organs, which the body must always patiently carry about; yes, which we must even nourish and minister to, glad if only they perform their functions properly?

Similarly God deals with us. Because He would confer eternal life upon man, He patiently endures the filthy righteousness of this life wherein we must dwell until the last day, for the sake of His chosen people and until the number is complete. For so long as the final day is deferred, not all to have eternal life are yet born. When the time shall be fulfilled, the number completed, God will suddenly bring to an end the world with its governments, its jurists and authorities, its conditions of life; in short, He will utterly abolish earthly righteousness, destroying physical appetites and all else together. For every form of human holiness is condemned to destruction; yet for the sake of Christians, to whom eternal life is appointed, and for their sake only, all these must be perpetuated until the last saint is born and has attained life everlasting. Were there but one saint yet to be born, for the sake of that one the world must remain. For God regards not the world nor has He need for it, except for the sake of His Christians.

Therefore, when God enjoins upon us obedience to the emperor, and godly, honest lives on earth, it is no warrant that our subjection to temporal authority is to continue forever. Instead, God necessarily will minister to, adorn and honor this wretched body—vile body, as Paul here has it—with power and dominion. Yet the apostle terms human righteousness "filth," and says it is not necessary to God's kingdom; indeed, that it is condemned in the sight of God with all its honor and glory, and all the world must be ashamed of it in his presence, confessing themselves guilty. Paul in Romans 3:27 and 4:2 testifies to this fact when he tells how even the exalted, holy fathers—Abraham, and others—though having glory before the world because of their righteous works, could not make them serve to obtain honor before God. Much less will worldly honor avail with God in the case of individuals who, being called honorable, pious, honest, virtuous—lords and princes, wives and husbands—boast of such righteousness.

From "Enemies of the Cross of Christ."

77

THE SAYING THAT, EVEN IF ST. PETER WERE NOW POPE, HE
COULD GRANT NO GREATER GRACES, IS BLASPHEMY AGAINST
ST. PETER AND THE POPE.

Faith...unites the soul to Christ, as the wife to the husband;
by which mystery, as the apostle teaches, Christ and the soul are
made one flesh. Now if they are one flesh, and if a true marriage—
nay, by far the most perfect of all marriages—is accomplished
between them (for human marriages are but feeble types of this
one great marriage), then it follows that all they have becomes
theirs in common, as well good things as evil things; so that whatsoever Christ possesses, that the believing soul may take to itself
and boast of as its own, and whatever belongs to the soul, that
Christ claims as His.

If we compare these possessions, we shall see how inestimable
is the gain. Christ is full of grace, life, and salvation; the soul is full
of sin, death, and condemnation. Let faith step in, and then sin,
death, and hell will belong to Christ, and grace, life, and salvation
to the soul. For, if He is a husband, He must needs take to Himself
that which is His wife's, and, at the same time, impart to His wife
that which is His. For, in giving her His own body and Himself,
how can He but give her all that is His? And, in taking to Himself

the body of His wife, how can He but take to Himself all that is hers?

In this is displayed the delightful sight, not only of communion, but of a prosperous warfare, of victory, salvation, and redemption. For since Christ is God and man, and is such a Person as neither has sinned, nor dies, nor is condemned,—nay, cannot sin, die, or be condemned; and since his righteousness, life, and salvation are invincible, eternal, and almighty; when, I say, such a Person, by the wedding ring of faith, takes a share in the sins, death, and hell of His wife, nay, makes them His own, and deals with them no otherwise than as if they were His, and as if He Himself had sinned; and when He suffers, dies, and descends to hell, that He may overcome all things, since sin, death, and hell cannot swallow Him up, they must needs be swallowed up by Him in stupendous conflict. For His righteousness rises above the sins of all men; His life is more powerful than all death; His salvation is more unconquerable than all hell.

Thus the believing soul, by the pledge of its faith in Christ, becomes free from all sin, fearless of death, safe from hell, and endowed with the eternal righteousness, life, and salvation of its husband Christ. Thus He presents to Himself a glorious bride, without spot or wrinkle, cleansing her with the washing of water by the Word; that is, by faith in the Word of life, righteousness, and salvation. Thus He betrothes her unto Himself "*in righteousness, and in judgment, and in lovingkindness, and in mercies*" (Hosea 2:19–20).

From "Concerning Christian Liberty."

78

W<small>E AFFIRM ON THE CONTRARY THAT BOTH HE AND ANY OTHER</small> <small>POPE HAS GREATER GRACES TO GRANT, NAMELY, THE GOSPEL,</small> <small>POWERS, GIFTS OF HEALING, ETC.</small> (S<small>EE</small> 1 C<small>ORINTHIANS</small> 12:9.)

Thus it cannot be true that there is inherent in the sacraments a power effectual to produce justification, or that they are efficacious signs of grace. These things are said in ignorance of the divine promise and to the great detriment of faith; unless indeed we call them efficacious in this sense, that, if along with them there be unhesitating faith, they do confer grace most certainly and most effectually. But that it is not this kind of efficacy that those writers attribute to them is evident from this, that they assert them to be profitable to all men, even the wicked and unbelieving, provided they put no obstacle in the way; as if unbelief itself were not the most persistent of all obstacles, and the most hostile to grace. Thus they have endeavored to make out of the sacrament a precept, and out of faith a work. For if a sacrament confers grace on me, merely because I receive it, then it is certainly by my own work and not by faith that I obtain grace; nor do I apprehend any promise in the sacrament, but only a sign instituted and commanded by God. It is evident from this how utterly the sacraments are misunderstood by these theologians of the Sentences, inasmuch as they make no account either of faith or of the promise in the sacraments, but cleave only to the sign and the use of the sign, and carry us away from faith to works, from the word to the sign. Thus, as I have said, they have not only brought the sacraments into bondage, but, as far as in them lay, have entirely done away with them.

Let us then open our eyes, and learn to look more to the Word than the sign, more to faith than to the work or use of the sign; and let us understand that wherever there is a divine promise, there faith is required; and that both of these are so necessary that neither can be of any effect without the other. We can neither believe unless we have a promise, nor is the promise effectual unless it is believed; while if these two act reciprocally, they produce a real and sure efficacy in the sacraments. Hence to seek efficacy in the sacrament independently of the promise and of faith is to strive in vain and to fall into condemnation. Thus Christ says: *"He that believeth and is baptized shall be saved; but he that believeth not shall be damned"* (Mark 16:16). Thus He shows that in the sacrament faith is so necessary that it can save us even without the sacrament; and on this account when He says: *"He that believeth not,"* He does not add: *"and is not baptized."*

From "On the Babylonish Captivity of the Church."

79

To say that the cross set up among the insignia of the papal arms is of equal power with the cross of Christ, is blasphemy.

The benefit of Christ's sufferings depends almost entirely upon man coming to a true knowledge of himself, and becoming terror-stricken and slain before himself. And where man does not come to this point, the sufferings of Christ have become of no true benefit to him. For the characteristic, natural work of Christ's sufferings is that they make all men equal and alike, so that as Christ was horribly martyred as to body and soul in our sins, we must also like Him be martyred in our consciences by our sins. This does not take place by means of many words, but by means of deep thoughts and a profound realization of our sins. Take an illustration: If an evil-doer were judged because he had slain the child of a prince or king, and you were in safety, and sang and played, as if you were entirely innocent, until one seized you in a horrible manner and convinced you that you had enabled the wicked person to do the act; behold, then you would be in the greatest straits, especially if your conscience also revolted against you. Thus much more anxious you should be, when you consider Christ's sufferings.

Whoever perceives himself to be so hard and sterile that he is not terror-stricken by Christ's sufferings and led to a knowledge of Him, he should fear and tremble. For it cannot be otherwise; you must become like the picture and sufferings of Christ, be it realized in life or in hell; you must at the time of death, if not sooner, fall into terror, tremble, quake, and experience all Christ suffered on the cross. It is truly terrible to attend to this on your deathbed; therefore you should pray God to soften your heart and permit you fruitfully to meditate upon Christ's Passion. For it is impossible for us profoundly to meditate upon the sufferings of Christ of ourselves, unless God sink them into our hearts. Further, neither this meditation nor any other doctrine is given to you to the end that you should fall fresh upon it of yourself, to accomplish the same; but you are first to seek and long for the grace of God, that you may accomplish it through God's grace and not through your own power. For in this way it happens that those referred to above never treat the sufferings of Christ aright; for they never call upon God to that end, but devise out of their own ability their own way, and treat those sufferings entirely in a human and an unfruitful manner.

From "Christ's Holy Sufferings."

80

THOSE BISHOPS, CURATES, AND THEOLOGIANS WHO ALLOW
SUCH DISCOURSES TO HAVE CURRENCY AMONG THE PEOPLE,
WILL HAVE TO RENDER AN ACCOUNT.

Since, then, we hold the name and title of teachers of the Holy
Scriptures, we should verily be forced to act according to our title,
and to teach the Holy Scriptures and nothing else. Although,
indeed, it is a proud, presumptuous title, for a man to proclaim himself teacher of the Scriptures, still it could be suffered, if the works
confirmed the title. But as it is, under the rule of the Sentences,
we find among theologians more human and heathenish fallacies
than true holy knowledge of the Scriptures. What then are we to
do? I know not, except to pray humbly to God to give us doctors
of theology. Doctors of arts, of medicine, of law, of the sentences,
may be made by popes, emperors and the universities; but of this
we may be certain, a doctor of the Holy Scriptures can be made by
none but the Holy Ghost, as Christ says: "They shall be all taught
of God" (John 6:45). Now the Holy Ghost does not consider red
caps or brown, or any other pomp; nor whether we are young or
old, layman or priest, monk or secular, virgin or married; nay, He
once spoke by an ass against the prophet that rode on it. Would
to God we were worthy of having such doctors given us, be they

laymen or priests, married or virgin! But now they try to force the Holy Ghost to enter into popes, bishops, or doctors, though there is no sign to show that He is in them....

Oh, how badly we treat all these poor young people that are entrusted to us for discipline and instruction! and a heavy reckoning shall we have to give for it that we keep them from the word of God; their fate is that described by Jeremiah: "Mine eyes do fail with tears, my bowels are troubled, my liver is poured upon the earth, for the destruction of the daughter of my people; because the children and the sucklings swoon in the streets of the city. They say to their mothers, Where is corn and wine? when they swooned as the wounded in the streets of the city, when their soul was poured out into their mothers' bosom" (Lamentations 2:11–12). We do not perceive all this misery, how the young folk are being pitifully corrupted in the midst of Christendom, all for want of the gospel, which we should always read and study with them.

From "To the Christian Nobility of the German Nation Respecting the Reformation of the Christian Faith."

THIS LICENSE IN THE PREACHING OF PARDONS MAKES IT NO
EASY THING, EVEN FOR LEARNED MEN, TO PROTECT THE REV-
ERENCE DUE TO THE POPE AGAINST THE CALUMNIES, OR, AT
ALL EVENTS, THE KEEN QUESTIONINGS OF THE LAITY.

Any man possessing this knowledge may easily keep clear of
danger among those innumerable commands and precepts of the
pope, of bishops, of monasteries, of churches, of princes, and of
magistrates, which some foolish pastors urge on us as being necessary for justification and salvation, calling them precepts of the
church, when they are not so at all. For the Christian freeman will
speak thus: I will fast, I will pray, I will do this or that, which is
commanded me by men, not as having any need of these things for
justification or salvation, but that I may thus comply with the will
of the pope, of the bishop, of such a community or such a magistrate, or of my neighbor as an example to him; for this cause I will
do and suffer all things, just as Christ did and suffered much more
for me, though He needed not at all to do so on His own account,
and made Himself for my sake under the law, when He was not
under the law. And although tyrants may do me violence or wrong
in requiring obedience to these things, yet it will not hurt me to do
them, so long as they are not done against God.

162

From all this every man will be able to attain a sure judgment and faithful discrimination between all works and laws, and to know who are blind and foolish pastors, and who are true and good ones. For whatsoever work is not directed to the sole end, either of keeping under the body, or of doing service to our neighbor—provided he require nothing contrary to the will of God—is no good or Christian work. Hence I greatly fear that at this day few or no colleges, monasteries, altars, or ecclesiastical functions are Christian ones; and the same may be said of fasts and special prayers to certain Saints. I fear that in all these nothing is being sought but what is already ours; while we fancy that by these things our sins are purged away and salvation is attained, and thus utterly do away with Christian liberty. This comes from ignorance of Christian faith and liberty.

From "Concerning Christian Liberty."

82

AS FOR INSTANCE: WHY DOES NOT THE POPE EMPTY PUR-
GATORY FOR THE SAKE OF MOST HOLY CHARITY AND OF THE
SUPREME NECESSITY OF SOULS—THIS BEING THE MOST JUST OF
ALL REASONS—IF HE REDEEMS AN INFINITE NUMBER OF SOULS
FOR THE SAKE OF THAT MOST FATAL THING MONEY, TO BE SPENT
ON BUILDING A BASILICA—THIS BEING A VERY SLIGHT REASON?

Therefore, Leo my Father[6], beware of listening to those sirens, who make you out to be not simply a man, but partly a God, so that you can command and require whatever you will. It will not happen so, nor will you prevail. You are the servant of servants, and, more than any other man, in a most pitiable and perilous position. Let not those men deceive you, who pretend that you are Lord of the world; who will not allow anyone to be a Christian without your authority; who babble of your having power over heaven, hell, and purgatory. These men are your enemies and are seeking your soul to destroy it, as Isaiah says: "My people, they that call thee blessed are themselves deceiving thee." (See Isaiah 3:12.) They are in error, who raise you above councils and the universal church. They are in error, who attribute to you alone the right of interpreting Scripture. All these men are seeking to set up their

---

6. Pope Leo X

own impieties in the church under your name, and alas! Satan has gained much through them in the time of your predecessors.

In brief, trust not in any who exalt you, but in those who humiliate you. For this is the judgment of God: *"He hath put down the mighty from their seats, and exalted them of low degree"* (Luke 1:52). See how unlike Christ was to His successors, though all will have it that they are His vicars. I fear that in truth very many of them have been in too serious a sense His vicars, for a vicar represents a prince who is absent. Now if a pontiff rules while Christ is absent and does not dwell in his heart, what else is he but a vicar of Christ? And then what is that church but a multitude without Christ? What indeed is such a vicar but Antichrist and an idol? How much more rightly did the apostles speak, who call themselves the servants of a present Christ, not the vicars of an absent one.

From "Concerning Christian Liberty."

83

Again; why do funeral masses and anniversary masses for the deceased continue, and why does not the pope return, or permit the withdrawal of the funds bequeathed for this purpose, since it is a wrong to pray for those who are already redeemed?

When the priest is performing mass publicly, let him understand that he is only receiving and giving to others the communion in the mass; and let him beware of offering up at the same moment his prayers for himself and others, lest he should seem to be presuming to offer the mass. The priest also who is saying a private mass must consider himself as administering the communion to himself. A private mass is not at all different from, nor more efficient than, the simple reception of the communion by any layman from the hand of the priest, except for the prayers, and that the priest consecrates and administers it to himself. In the matter itself of the mass and the sacrament, we are all equal, priests and laymen.

Even if he is requested by others to do so, let him beware of celebrating votive masses—as they are called—and of receiving any payment for the mass, or presuming to offer any votive sacrifice; but let him carefully refer all this to the prayers which he offers, whether for the dead or the living. Let him think thus:—I will go and receive the sacrament for myself alone, but while I receive it I will pray for this or that person, and thus, for purposes of food and clothing, receive payment for my prayers, and not for the mass. Nor let it shake thee in this view, though the whole world is of the contrary opinion and practice. You have the most certain authority of the gospel, and relying on this, you may easily contemn the ideas and opinions of men. If however, in despite of what I say, you will persist in offering the mass, and not your prayers only, then know that I have faithfully warned you, and that I shall stand clear in the day of judgment, while you will bear your own sin. I have said what I was bound to say to you, as a brother to a brother, for your salvation; it will be to your profit if you take heed to my words, to your hurt if you neglect them. And if there are some who will condemn these statements of mine, I reply in the words of Paul: *"Evil men and seducers shall wax worse and worse, deceiving, and being deceived"* (2 Timothy 3:13).

From "On the Babylonish Captivity of the Church."

84

AGAIN; WHAT IS THIS NEW KINDNESS OF GOD AND THE POPE, IN THAT, FOR MONEY'S SAKE, THEY PERMIT AN IMPIOUS MAN AND AN ENEMY OF GOD TO REDEEM A PIOUS SOUL WHICH LOVES GOD, AND YET DO NOT REDEEM THAT SAME PIOUS AND BELOVED SOUL, OUT OF FREE CHARITY, ON ACCOUNT OF ITS OWN NEED?

All heretics have continually failed in this one point, that they do not rightly understand or know the article of justification. If we had not this article certain and clear, it were impossible we could criticize the pope's false doctrine of indulgences and other abominable errors, much less be able to overcome greater spiritual errors and vexations. If we only permit Christ to be our Savior, then we have won, for He is the only girdle that clasps the whole body together, as St. Paul excellently teaches. If we look to the spiritual birth and substance of a true Christian, we shall soon extinguish all deserts of good works; for they serve us to no use, neither to purchase sanctification, nor to deliver us from sin, death, devil, or hell.

Little children are saved only by faith, without any good works; therefore faith alone justifies. If God's power be able to effect that in one, then He is also able to accomplish it in all; for the power of the child effects it not, but the power of faith; neither is it done through the child's weakness or disability; for then that weakness would be merit of itself, or equivalent to merit. It is a mischievous thing that we miserable, sinful wretches will upbraid God, and hit Him in the teeth with our works, and think thereby to be justified before Him; but God will not allow it.

This article, how we are saved, is the chief of the whole Christian doctrine, to which all divine disputations must be directed. All the prophets were chiefly engaged upon it, and sometimes much perplexed about it. For when this article is kept fast and sure by a constant faith, then all other articles draw on softly after, as that of the Holy Trinity, etc. God has declared no article so plainly and openly as this, that we are saved only by Christ; though He speaks much of the Holy Trinity, yet He dwells continually upon this article of the salvation of our souls; other articles are of great weight, but this surpasses all.

From *Table Talk*.

85

AGAIN; WHY IS IT THAT THE PENITENTIAL CANONS, LONG
SINCE ABROGATED AND DEAD IN THEMSELVES IN VERY FACT
AND NOT ONLY BY USAGE, ARE YET STILL REDEEMED WITH
MONEY, THROUGH THE GRANTING OF INDULGENCES, AS IF
THEY WERE FULL OF LIFE?

O would that, having laid aside that glory which your most
abandoned enemies declare to be yours, you were living rather in
the office of a private priest, or on your paternal inheritance! In
that glory none are worthy to glory, except the race of Iscariot,
the children of perdition. For what happens in your court, Leo,
except that, the more wicked and execrable any man is, the more
prosperously he can use your name and authority for the ruin of
the property and souls of men, for the multiplication of crimes, for
the oppression of faith and truth, and of the whole church of God?
O Leo! in reality most unfortunate, and sitting on a most perilous
throne—I tell you the truth, because I wish you well; for if Bernard
felt compassion for his Anastasius at a time when the Roman See,
though even then most corrupt, was as yet ruling with better hope
than now, why should not we lament, to whom so much additional
corruption and ruin has happened in three hundred years?

Is it not true that there is nothing under the vast heavens more corrupt, more pestilential, more hateful than the Court of Rome? She incomparably surpasses the impiety of the Turks, so that in very truth she, who was formerly the gate of heaven, is now a sort of open mouth of hell, and such a mouth as, under the urgent wrath of God, cannot be blocked up; one course alone being left to us wretched men, to call back and save some few, if we can, from that Roman gulf.

From "Concerning Christian Liberty."

86

AGAIN; WHY DOES NOT THE POPE, WHOSE RICHES ARE AT THIS DAY MORE AMPLE THAN THOSE OF THE WEALTHIEST OF THE WEALTHY, BUILD THE ONE BASILICA OF ST. PETER WITH HIS OWN MONEY, RATHER THAN WITH THAT OF POOR BELIEVERS?

The Roman See must abolish the papal offices, and diminish that crowd of crawling vermin at Rome, so that the pope's servants may be supported out of the pope's own pocket, and that his court may cease to surpass all royal courts in its pomp and extravagance; seeing that all this pomp has not only been of no service to the Christian faith, but has also kept them from study and prayer, so that they themselves know hardly anything concerning matters of faith; as they proved clumsily enough at the last Roman Council, where among many childishly trifling matters, they decided "that the soul is immortal," and that a priest is bound to pray once every month on pain of losing his benefice. How are men to rule Christendom and to decide matters of faith, who, callous and blinded by their greed, wealth, and worldly pomp, have only just decided that the soul is immortal? It is no slight shame to all Christendom that they should deal thus scandalously with the faith at Rome. If they had less wealth and lived in less pomp, they might be better able to study and pray, that they might become able and worthy to treat matters of belief, as they were once, when they were content to be bishops and not kings of kings.

The terrible oaths must be abolished which bishops are forced, without any right, to swear to the pope, by which they are bound like servants, and which are arbitrarily and foolishly decreed in the absurd and shallow chapter, Significasti. Is it not enough that they oppress us in goods, body, and soul by all their mad laws, by which they have weakened faith and destroyed Christianity; but must they now take possession of the very persons of bishops, with their offices and functions, and also claim the investiture that used formerly to be the right of the German emperors, and is still the right of the king in France and other kingdoms? This matter caused many wars and disputes with the emperors until the popes impudently took the power by force; since which time they have retained it; just as if it were only right for the Germans, above all Christians on earth, to be the fools of the pope and the Holy See, and to do and suffer what no one beside would suffer or do. Seeing then that this is mere arbitrary power, robbery, and a hindrance to the exercise of the bishop's ordinary power, and to the injury of poor souls; therefore it is the duty of the emperor and his nobles to prevent and punish this tyranny.

From "To the Christian Nobility of the German Nation Respecting the Reformation of the Christian Estate."

87

AGAIN; WHAT DOES THE POPE REMIT OR IMPART TO THOSE
WHO, THROUGH PERFECT CONTRITION, HAVE A RIGHT TO PLE-
NARY REMISSION AND PARTICIPATION?

As therefore a wicked man can baptize, that is, can apply the
word of promise and the sign of water to the person baptized, so
can he also apply and minister the promise of this sacrament to
those who partake of it, and partake himself with them, as the
traitor Judas did in the supper of the Lord. Still the sacrament
and testament remains always the same; it performs in the believer
its own proper work, in the unbeliever it performs a work foreign
to itself. But in the matter of oblations the case is quite different;
for since it is not the mass but prayers that are offered to God, it
is evident that the oblations of a wicked priest are of no value. As
Gregory himself says, when we employ an unworthy person as an
advocate, the mind of the judge is prejudiced against us. We must
not therefore confound these two things, the mass and prayer, sacrament and work, testament and sacrifice. The one comes from
God to us through the ministry of the priest, and requires faith on
our part; the other goes forth from our faith to God through the
priest, and requires that He should hear us; the one comes down,
the other goes upward. The one, therefore, does not necessarily

require that the minister should be worthy and pious, but the other does require it, because God does not hear sinners. He knows how to do us good by means of wicked men, but He does not accept the works of any wicked man, as He showed in the case of Cain. It is written: "*The sacrifice of the wicked is an abomination to the* L<small>ORD</small>" (Proverbs 15:8); and again: "*Whatsoever is not of faith is sin*" (Romans 14:23).

I am ready to produce further arguments when anyone comes forward to attack these. From all that has been said we see for whom the mass was intended, and who are worthy partakers of it; namely, those alone who have sad, afflicted, disturbed, confused, and erring consciences. For since the word of the divine promise in this sacrament holds forth to us remission of sins, any man may safely draw near to it who is harassed either by remorse for sin, or by temptation to sin. This testament of Christ is the one medicine for past, present, and future sins; provided you cleave to it with unhesitating faith, and believe that that which is signified by the Words of the testament is freely given to you. If you do not believe, then nowhere, never, by no works, by no efforts, will you be able to appease your conscience. For faith is the sole peace of conscience, and unbelief the sole disturber of conscience.

From "On the Babylonish Captivity of the Church."

AGAIN; WHAT GREATER GOOD WOULD THE CHURCH RECEIVE
IF THE POPE, INSTEAD OF ONCE, AS HE DOES NOW, WERE TO
BESTOW THESE REMISSIONS AND PARTICIPATIONS A HUNDRED
TIMES A DAY ON ANY ONE OF THE FAITHFUL?

The gospel of the remission of sins through faith in Christ, is received of few people; most men little regard the sweet and comfortable tidings of the gospel; some hear it, but only even so as they hear mass in popedom; the majority attend God's Word out of custom, and, when they have done that, think all is well. The case is, the sick, needing a physician, welcome him; but he that is well, cares not for him, as we see by the Canaanitish woman in Matthew 15, who felt her own and her daughter's necessities, and therefore ran after Christ, and in nowise would suffer herself to be denied or sent away from Him. In like manner, Moses was fain to go before, and learn to feel sins, that so grace might taste the sweeter. Therefore, it is but labor lost (how familiar and loving soever Christ be figured unto us), except we first be humbled through the acknowledgment of our sins, and so yearn after Christ, as the Magnificat says: *"He hath filled the hungry with good things; and the rich he hath sent empty away"* (Luke 1:53), words spoken for the comfort of all, and for instruction of miserable, poor, needful sinners, and condemned people, to the end that in all their deepest sorrows and necessities they may know with whom to take refuge and seek aid and consolation.

But we must take fast hold on God's Word, and believe all true which that says of God, though God and all his creatures should seem unto us other than as the Word speaks, as we see the Canaanite woman did. The Word is sure, and fails not, though heaven and earth must pass away. Yet, oh! how hard is this to natural sense and reason, that it must strip itself naked, and abandon all it comprehends and feels, depending only upon the bare Word. The Lord of his mercy help us with faith in our necessities, and at our last end, when we strive with death.

From *Table Talk*.

89

SINCE IT IS THE SALVATION OF SOULS, RATHER THAN MONEY, THAT THE POPE SEEKS BY HIS PARDONS, WHY DOES HE SUS-PEND THE LETTERS AND PARDONS GRANTED LONG AGO, SINCE THEY ARE EQUALLY EFFICACIOUS.

Wicked men create a great opinion of their own inventions, and puff up human works, in order to allure the senseless multitude, who are easily led by a specious show of works; to the great ruin of faith, forgetfulness of baptism, and injury to Christian liberty. As a vow is a sort of law and requires a work, it follows that, as vows are multiplied, so laws and works are multiplied; and by the multiplication of these, faith is extinguished, and the liberty of baptism is brought into bondage. Not content with these impious allurements, others go further, and assert that entrance into a religious order is like a new baptism, which may be successively renewed, as often as the purpose of a religious life is renewed. Thus these devotees attribute to themselves alone righteousness, salvation, and glory, and leave to the baptized absolutely no room for comparison with them. The Roman pontiff, that fountain and author of all superstitions, confirms, approves, and embellishes these ideas by grandly worded bulls and indulgences; while no one thinks baptism worthy even of mention. By these showy displays they drive the easily led people of Christ into whatever whirlpools of error they will; so that, unthankful for their baptism, they imagine that they can do better by their works than others by their faith.

Wherefore God also, who is froward with the forward (see Psalm 18:26), resolving to avenge Himself on the pride and unthankfulness of these devotees, causes them either to fail in keeping their vows, or to keep them with great labor and to continue immersed in them, never becoming acquainted with the grace of faith and of baptism. As their spirit is not right with God, He permits them to continue to the end in their hypocrisy, and to become at length a laughing stock to the whole world, always following after righteousness, and never attaining to it; so that they fulfil that saying: *"Their land also is full of idols"* (Isaiah 2:8).

I should certainly not forbid or object to any vow that a man may make of his own private choice. I do not wish altogether to condemn or depreciate vows; but my advice would be altogether against the public establishment or confirmation of any such mode of life. It is enough that every man should be at liberty to make private vows at his own peril; but that a public system of living under the constraint of vows should be inculcated, I consider to be a thing pernicious to the church and to all simple souls. In the first place, it is not a little repugnant to the Christian life, inasmuch as a vow is a kind of ceremonial law, and a matter of human tradition or invention; from all that the church has been set free by baptism, since the Christian is bound by no law, except that of God. Moreover there is no example of it in the Scriptures, especially of the vow of perpetual chastity, obedience, and poverty. Now a vow of which we have no example in the Scriptures is a perilous one, which ought to be urged upon no man, much less be established as a common and public mode of life; even if every individual must be allowed to venture upon it at his own peril, if he will. There are some works which are wrought by the Spirit in but few, and these ought by no means to be brought forward as an example, or as a manner of life.

From "On the Babylonian Captivity of the Church."

90

To REPRESS THESE SCRUPLES AND ARGUMENTS OF THE LAITY BY FORCE ALONE, AND NOT TO SOLVE THEM BY GIVING REASONS, IS TO EXPOSE THE CHURCH AND THE POPE TO THE RIDICULE OF THEIR ENEMIES, AND TO MAKE CHRISTIAN MEN UNHAPPY.

No sinner can escape his punishment, unless he be sorry for his sins. For though one go scot-free for a while, yet at last he will be snapped, as the Psalm says: *"Verily he is a God that judgeth in the earth"* (Psalm 58:11). Our Lord God suffers the ungodly to be surprised and taken captive in very slight and small things, when they think not of it, when they are most secure, and live in delight and pleasure, leaping for joy. In such manner was the pope surprised by me, about his indulgences and pardons, comparatively a slight matter.

A magistrate, a father or mother, a master or dame, tradesmen and others, must now and then look through the fingers at their citizens, children, and servants, if their faults and offenses be not too gross and frequent; for where we will have *summum jus*,[7] there follows often *summa injuria*,[8] so that all must go to wreck. Neither

---

7. "extreme right"
8. "exteme injury"

do they that are in office always hit it aright, but err and sin themselves, and must therefore desire the forgiveness of sins.

God forgives sins merely out of grace for Christ's sake; but we must not abuse the grace of God. God has given signs and tokens enough, that our sins shall be forgiven; namely, the preaching of the gospel, baptism, the Lord's Supper, and the Holy Ghost in our hearts.

Now it is also needful we testify in our works that we have received the forgiveness of sins, by each forgiving the faults of his brother. There is no comparison between God's remitting of sins and ours. For what are one hundred pence, in comparison with ten thousand pounds? As Christ says, naught. And although we deserve nothing by our forgiving, yet we must forgive that thereby we may prove and give testimony that we from God have received forgiveness of our sins.

The forgiveness of sins is declared only in God's Word, and there we must seek it; for it is grounded on God's promises. God forgives you your sins, not because you feel them and are sorry, for this sin itself produces, without deserving, but He forgives your sins because He is merciful, and because He has promised to forgive for Christ's sake.

From *Table Talk*.

91

IF THEN PARDONS WERE PREACHED ACCORDING TO THE SPIRIT AND MIND OF THE POPE, ALL THESE QUESTIONS WOULD BE RESOLVED WITH EASE; NAY, WOULD NOT EXIST.

An understanding of practically all of the epistle to the Hebrews is necessary before we can hope to make this text clear to ourselves. Briefly, the epistle treats of a twofold priesthood. The former priesthood was a material one, with material adornment, tabernacle, sacrifices, and with pardon couched in ritual; material were all its appointments. The new order is a spiritual priesthood, with spiritual adornments, spiritual tabernacle and sacrifices—spiritual in all that pertains to it. Christ, in the exercise of his priestly office, in the sacrifice on the cross, was not adorned with silk and gold and precious stones, but with divine love, wisdom, patience, obedience and all virtues. His adornment was apparent to none but God and possessors, of the Spirit, for it was spiritual.

Christ sacrificed not goats nor calves nor birds; not bread; not blood nor flesh, as did Aaron and his posterity: He offered his own body and blood, and the manner of the sacrifice was spiritual; for it took place through the Holy Spirit, as here stated. Though the body and blood of Christ were visible the same as any other material object, the fact that He offered them as a sacrifice was not apparent. It was not a visible sacrifice, as in the case of offerings at the hands of Aaron. Then the goat or calf, the flesh and blood, were material sacrifices visibly offered, and recognized as sacrifices. But Christ offered Himself in the heart before God. His sacrifice was perceptible to no mortal. Therefore, His bodily flesh and blood becomes a spiritual sacrifice. Similarly, we Christians, the posterity of Christ our Aaron, offer up our own bodies. (See Romans 12:1.) And our offering is likewise a spiritual sacrifice, or, as Paul has it, a "reasonable service"; for we make it in spirit, and it is beheld of God alone.

Again, in the new order, the tabernacle or house is spiritual; for it is heaven, or the presence of God. Christ hung upon a cross; He was not offered in a temple. He was offered before the eyes of God, and there He still abides. The cross is an altar in a spiritual sense. The material cross was indeed visible, but none knew it as Christ's altar. Again, His prayer, His sprinkled blood, His burnt incense, were all spiritual, for it was all wrought through His spirit.

From "Christ Our Great High Priest."

92

AWAY THEN WITH ALL THOSE PROPHETS WHO SAY TO THE
PEOPLE OF CHRIST, "PEACE, PEACE," AND THERE IS NO PEACE.

Others, far more shamelessly, arrogate to the pope the power of
making laws; arguing from the words: *"Whatsoever thou shalt bind
on earth shall be bound in heaven; and whatsoever thou shalt loose on
earth shall be loosed in heaven"* (Matthew 16:19). Christ is speaking there of the binding and loosing of sins, not of bringing the
whole church into bondage and making laws to oppress it. Thus
the papal tyranny acts in all things on its own false maxims; while
it forcibly wrests and perverts the words of God. I admit indeed
that Christians must endure this accursed tyranny, as they would
any other violence inflicted on them by the world, according to the
saying of Christ: *"Whosoever shall smite thee on thy right cheek, turn
to him the other also"* (Matthew 5:39). But I complain of this, that
wicked pontiffs boast that they have a rightful power to act thus,
and pretend that in this Babylon of theirs they are providing for the
interests of Christendom; an idea that they have persuaded all men
to adopt. If they did these things in conscious and avowed impiety and tyranny, or if it were simple violence that we endured, we
might meanwhile quietly reckon up the advantages thus afforded us
for the mortification of this life and the fulfillment of baptism, and
should retain the full right of glorying in conscience at the wrong

done us. As it is, they desire so to ensnare our consciences in the matter of liberty that we should believe all that they do to be well done, and should think it unlawful to blame or complain of their iniquitous actions. Being wolves, they wish to appear shepherds; being antichrists, they wish to be honored like Christ.

I cry aloud on behalf of liberty and conscience, and I proclaim with confidence that no kind of law can with any justice be imposed on Christians, whether by men or by angels, except so far as they themselves will; for we are free from all. If such laws are imposed on us, we ought so to endure them as still to preserve the consciousness of our liberty. We ought to know and steadfastly to protest that a wrong is being done to that liberty, though we may bear and even glory in that wrong; taking care neither to justify the tyrant nor to murmur against the tyranny. "*Who is he that will harm you, if ye be followers of that which is good?*" (1 Peter 3:13). All things work together for good to the elect of God. Since, however, there are but few who understand the glory of baptism and the happiness of Christian liberty, or who can understand them for the tyranny of the pope—I for my part will set free my own mind and deliver my conscience, by declaring aloud to the pope and to all papists, that, unless they shall throw aside all their laws and traditions, and restore liberty to the churches of Christ, and cause that liberty to be taught, they are guilty of the death of all the souls which are perishing in this wretched bondage, and that the papacy is in truth nothing else than the kingdom of Babylon and of very antichrist. For who is the man of sin and the son of perdition, but he who by his teaching and his ordinances increases the sin and perdition of souls in the church; while he yet sits in the church as if he were God? All these conditions have now for many ages been fulfilled by the papal tyranny. It has extinguished faith, darkened the sacraments, crushed the gospel; while it has enjoined and multiplied without end its own laws, which are not only wicked and sacrilegious, but also most unlearned and barbarous.

From "On the Babylonian Captivity of the Church."

93

BLESSED BE ALL THOSE PROPHETS, WHO SAY TO THE PEOPLE OF CHRIST: "THE CROSS, THE CROSS," AND THERE IS NO CROSS.

In this matter let every man be fully persuaded in his own mind. I shall carry out my undertaking, and speak on behalf of the liberty of the church and of the glory of baptism; and I shall state for the general benefit what I have learnt under the teaching of the Spirit. And first I counsel those who are in high places in the church to do away with all those vows and the practice of living under vows, or, at the least, not to approve or extol them. If they will not do this, then I earnestly advise all who desire to make their salvation the safer—particularly growing youths and young men—to keep aloof from all vows, especially from such as are extensive and life-long. I give this advice in the first place because this mode of life, as I have already said, has no evidence or example in the Scriptures, but rests only on the bulls of the pontiffs, who are but men; and second, because it tends to lead men into hypocrisy through its singularity and showy appearance, whence arise pride and contempt of the ordinary Christian life. If there were no other cause for doing away with these vows, this one by itself would have weight enough, that by them faith and baptism are depreciated, and works are magnified. Now these cannot be magnified without ruinous consequences, for among many thousands there is scarcely one who does not look more to his works as a member of a religious order, than to faith; and under this delusion they claim superiority over each other as being stricter or laxer, as they call it.

Hence I advise no man, yea, I dissuade every man from entering into the priesthood or any religious order, unless he be so fortified with knowledge as to understand that, however sacred and lofty may be the works of priests or of the religious orders, they differ not at all in the sight of God from the works of a husbandman laboring in his field, or of a woman attending to her household affairs, but that in His eyes all things are measured by faith alone. Nay, it very often happens that the common work of a servant or a handmaiden is more acceptable to God than all the fasting and works of a monk or a priest, when they are done without faith. Since, then, it is likely that at the present day vows only tend to increase men's pride and presumption in their own works, it is to be feared that there is nowhere less of faith and of the church than in priests, monks, and bishops; and that these very men are really Gentiles and hypocrites, who consider themselves to be the church, or the very heart of the church, spiritual persons, and rulers of the church, when they are very far indeed from being so. These are really the people of the captivity, among whom all the free gifts bestowed in baptism have been brought into bondage; while the poor and slender remnant of the people of the land appear vile in their eyes.

From "On the Babylonian Captivity of the Church."

94

CHRISTIANS SHOULD BE EXHORTED TO STRIVE TO FOLLOW
CHRIST THEIR HEAD THROUGH PAINS, DEATHS, AND HELLS.

I dare say I have sung a lofty strain, that I have proposed many things that will be thought impossible, and attacked many points too sharply. But what was I to do? I was bound to say this: if I had the power, this is what I would do. I had rather incur the world's anger than God's; they cannot take from me more than my life. I have hitherto made many offers of peace to my adversaries. But, as I see, God has forced me through them to open my mouth wider and wider, and, because they do not keep quiet, to give them enough cause for speaking, barking, shouting and writing. Well, then, I have another song still to sing concerning them and Rome; if they wish to hear it, I will sing it to them, and sing with all my might. Do you understand, my friend Rome, what I mean?

I have frequently offered to submit my writings for inquiry and examination, but in vain; though I know, if I am in the right, I must be condemned upon earth, and justified by Christ alone in heaven. For all the Scriptures teach us, that the affairs of Christians and Christendom must be judged by God alone; they have never yet been justified by men in this world, but the opposition has always been too strong. My greatest care and fear is, lest my cause be not condemned by men; by which I should know for certain that it does not please God. Therefore let them go freely to work, pope, bishop, priest, monk, or doctor; they are the true people to persecute the truth, as they have always done. May God grant us all a Christian understanding, and especially to the Christian nobility of the German nation true spiritual courage, to do what is best for our unhappy church. Amen!

From "To the Christian Nobility of the German Nation Respecting the Reformation of the Christian Faith."

95

AND THUS TRUST TO ENTER HEAVEN THROUGH MANY TRIBU-
LATIONS, RATHER THAN IN THE SECURITY OF PEACE.

I shall here make an end of this essay, which I readily and joyfully offer to all pious persons, who long to understand Scripture
in its sincere meaning, and to learn the genuine use of the sacraments. It is a gift of no slight importance to *"know the things that are
freely given to us of God"* (1 Corinthians 2:12), and to know in what
manner we ought to use those gifts. For if we are instructed in this
judgment of the Spirit, we shall not deceive ourselves by leaning
on those things that are opposed to it. Whereas our theologians
have not only nowhere given us the knowledge of these things, but
have even darkened them, as if of set purpose, I, if I have not given
that knowledge, have at least succeeded in not darkening it, and
have given others an inducement to think out something better. It
has at least been my endeavor to explain the meaning of both sacraments, but we cannot all do all things. On those impious men,
however, who in their obstinate tyranny press on us their own
teachings as if they were God's, I thrust these things freely and
confidently, caring not at all for their ignorance and violence. And
yet even to them I will wish sounder sense, and will not despise
their efforts, but will only distinguish them from those that are
legitimate and really Christian.

I hear a report that fresh bulls and papal curses are being prepared against me, by which I am to be urged to recant, or else be declared a heretic. If this is true, I wish this little book to be a part of my future recantation, that they may not complain that their tyranny has puffed itself up in vain. The remaining part I shall shortly publish, Christ being my helper, and that of such a sort as the See of Rome has never yet seen or heard, thus abundantly testifying my obedience in the name of our Lord Jesus Christ. Amen.

From "On the Babylonish Captivity of the Church."

ABOUT THE AUTHOR

Martin Luther (1483–1546) was one of Western history's most significant figures. After his studies at the University of Erfurt, this son of a copper miner became an Augustinian friar and was ordained in 1507. He taught at the University of Wittenberg, where he was made a doctor of Theology. In 1510, Luther visited Rome and was appalled by the corruption he found there. He became increasingly angry about the clergy selling "indulgences"—the sale of promised remission from the punishment for sins. In 1517, Luther published his "95 Theses," attacking papal abuses and the sale of indulgences. His work propounded two central beliefs: that the Bible is the central religious authority and that humans may reach salvation only by their faith and not by their deeds. Thanks to the recent invention of the printing press, "95 Theses" and his subsequent writings spread throughout Europe and became the spark of the Protestant Reformation. Although these ideas had been advanced before, Martin Luther codified them at a moment in history ripe for religious reformation. In 1521, Luther was excommunicated from the church and went into hiding at Wartburg Castle. In 1525, he married Katharina von Bora, a former nun, with whom he had six children. In 1534, Luther published a complete translation of the Bible into German, underlining his believe that people should be able to read it in their own language.